THE FIRST MAJOR VOLUME OF ST. PAUL HISTORY IN 63 YEARS

Much of the information within this book was first printed
as a daily column in the *St. Paul Dispatch* from December 2,
1974 to August 6, 1975, under the title: *"The Street Where
You Live."* For permission of the *St. Paul Dispatch* to use
their title and logo, I am grateful.

This book may be purchased from your
local bookseller, or from:

     Witsend Press
     1809 Stanford Avenue
     St. Paul, MN 55105

The price is $4.95.

The Street Where You Live

a guide to the street names of st. paul
by Donald Empson

Witsend Press: 1975: St. Paul

First Edition

copyright © *1975 by Donald Empson*
all rights reserved

Library of Congress catalog number: 75-37580

Library of Congress Cataloging in Publication Data

Empson, Donald Lawrence, 1942-
    The street where you live; a guide to the street
names of St. Paul.

    Includes index.
    1. Street names—Minnesota—St. Paul. 2. St.
Paul—Streets. I. Title.
F614.S4E46   917.76'581   75-37580

Dedicated
to
the

CURIOUS

of
whatever
size,
shape,
color,
sex,
or
age.

PREFACE

In this book, I have attempted to indicate the date and significance of all the street names presently in use within the city limits of St. Paul. Because any one street may have had several different names along its length at some time in the past, I have only indicated when the present name was first applied. To have listed every street name used in the city, and show what portion of the present street had that name, would be impossible. Not only are the records inaccurate, but the sheer volume of names--close to 6,000--is staggering.

When the significance of the street name was not obvious, or when I could not make a reasonably certain assumption, I did not guess at its meaning. Thus, Niagara Street might well refer to Niagara Falls, but I do not know. My experience has proven even the best of guesses wrong.

Although some persons seem skeptical, all the streets named in this book appear on the official map of St. Paul, compiled and distributed by the Department of Public Works. Because a few of the streets are not graded or marked, they are difficult to locate without the official map, but I have included them because they may be opened in the future.

The research for this book required over two years of often mind-numbing detail and persistence. I forced myself to recheck and resolve every point that was in doubt. The result is, I hope, a book of unusual accuracy, but I am too realistic to suppose it is entirely without error.

INTRODUCTION

how streets are named

Streets are usually named by the owner of the property on
which they occur. The developer--or proprietor--purchases
one or several acres to divide into building lots. He must
also provide land for a street to allow access to each
building lot. This division into building lots and streets
is known variously as a development, or a subdivision, or
an addition. The official map of this divided property is
called a plat; the act of surveying and drawing up such a
plat is called platting the property.

The developer is at liberty to bestow any name he wishes
upon the streets within his property, as long as it is not
obscene, overly long, difficult to spell or pronounce, a
duplicate of another name already used within the city, or
will not in any way be confused with another name already
in use. If the developer's new street happens to fall in
a line with another street already named, the previous
name must be extended within his property. All plats,
with their building lot dimensions and street names, must
be accepted by the city Plat Commission.

Neither the significance, aptness, originality, aesthetics,
history, nor any other consideration that would result in
an appropriate street name is taken into account. Thus we
have such misnomers as College Avenue with no college,
Palace Avenue with no palace, Ocean Street with no ocean,
and Hunting Valley Road with no valley. We also have well
over a hundred street names which are totally without
meaning, names like Fairview Avenue, Ashland Avenue,
Clifton Street, Hillcrest Avenue, Oakridge Street and the
like; street names which could be--and are--applied anywhere.

In a few instances, particularly in recent years, the developer will not include a street name upon his plat. This
void has often been filled by someone with the Department
of Public Works, or a member of the Plat Commission, who
will slip in the name of his wife, daughter, friend, or
whomever. Names applied in this manner, such as Leone
Avenue, or Jayne Street, or David Street, are very elusive
to trace.

On occasion the city itself will act as the developer of property they own. In that case, someone within the city offices will supply names they feel are significant-- usually those of other city officials.

Ultimate authority to accept or change street names within the city lies with the City Council who will usually approve without question the recommendations of the Plat Commission.

why streets are renamed

In the early decades of St. Paul, each developer, free to purchase property anywhere in the growing city, laid out his building lots and streets without regard for any master plan; indeed, without regard even for what the adjacent developer might be doing. Thus as the city compacted, and one development came to border another, the streets were found to have different names every few blocks; the streets were not aligned; they intersected each other at peculiar angles; and, in general, every developer's eccentricities confused the poor resident intent upon traveling from one part of the city to another.

The City Council could do little about the fact the streets were not always in straight lines, and everyone living in St. Paul today can think of instances where they have come to the end of one street and had to jog left or right to continue on that same street. However, the Council could ensure that every street running in more or less the same line would at least have the same name. So, for example, what was once St. Clair Street between Western Avenue and West Seventh Street, and Ludwig Avenue between West Seventh Street and Lexington Parkway, and Reserve Street between Snelling Avenue and Fairview Avenue, were eventually all brought under the original name: St. Clair Avenue.

The first streets in St. Paul, those of the downtown area, were named in 1847 and legally accepted in 1849. The first name change came nine years later, in 1858, when the City Council altered the names of Bench Street and St. Anthony Avenue, between Wabasha Street and Seven Corners, to Third Street (later Kellogg Boulevard).

The first major renaming of streets within the city oc- curred in 1872. At that time there were a number of duplicate street names: three John streets, for example, and four College streets. The impetus for change came from the Post Office which, in instituting the home delivery of mail, insisted there be only one street of each name within the city. It was also in 1872, perhaps for this same reason, that the city put up its first street name signs.

The second extensive renaming of streets happened in the decade following 1874 when the West Side, previously a separate town in Dakota County, was annexed to St. Paul and Ramsey County. This annexation brought a number of duplicate street names to the city map; all had to be changed to adhere to the policy of having only one street of each name.

The third substantial renaming took place in 1940 when the city planning department made another concerted effort to eliminate duplicate or duplicate sounding names, to ensure that the whole length of a street had the same name, and to reduce the frequent use of the same element (Como, for example) in several different street names. The department also tried to provide that East-West streets would be designated Avenues, that North-South streets would be designated Streets, and that diagonal streets would be called Roads. Traditional usage, however, created so many exceptions to this rule that the pattern is barely discernible, and certainly not to be relied upon.

While these particular years saw the renaming of dozens of streets, hardly a year has passed in which a few street names have not been changed. Unfortunately, not all the changes have been well intentioned or necessary.

The City Council, in acting upon street name changes, has catered to individuals (Aida Place), to companies (Wall Street), and to organizations (Grand Hill). At best these changes only perpetuate confusion and proliferate records; at worst, they replace a truly significant name with one of little or no meaning.

the quality of our street names

The careful selection and use of street names is, almost without exception, ignored. Yet they constitute, after an individual's name, the most important element of his identification. They greet every visitor to the city, appear on each of the thousands of pieces of mail coming into and leaving the city every day, are referred to around the world, and are used by every resident of the city on the average of three or four times a week.

The street names of St. Paul, like those of every city, are lacking in creativity. With a couple of notable exceptions like John E. Warren's Mt. Ida Street and John Wann's Saratoga Street, the street names are common, predictable, and without humor. There is no Easy Street to grace the city; no Intercourse Avenue to enliven the map; no What Street (What Street do you live on) to foster giggles. Where was the developer with the nerve to name his addition the Urinary Tract, with streets such as Kidney Lane, and Prostate Drive? Why did the city change the name of Teepeola Avenue (a word indicating many teepees), and why has Argue Street vanished from the city records? Why are there no streets named for herbs, colors, or zodiac signs?

Let there be a common sentiment between developers and city officials that street names, if possible, have some basic relationship with the land they occupy, acknowledging either the name of some individual associated with the property, or as a reminder of some striking and unusual geographic feature. Let there be an official policy that the merest suggestion of any street name containing the words: oak, hill, view, fair, pine, mont, wood, ridge, dale, crest, grove, hurst, land, park, edge, glen, high, or valley will automatically incur a fine of not less than $100, and at least a month in the workhouse.

previous writing on the street names

The only extensive information on the street names of St. Paul appeared in a volume by Warren Upham: <u>Minnesota Geographic Names; Their Origin and Historic Significance</u>. This book, containing thirty-one pages of research on the street and park names of St. Paul, was published in 1920 by the Minnesota Historical Society who reprinted the book in 1969. Much of the data gathered by Upham was featured in an extensive newspaper article in the <u>St. Paul Daily News</u> of March 1, 1925.

From time to time, an article was printed in the newspaper listing some of the obvious street name derivations, such as Ramsey Street or Sibley Street. Examples of this type of feature appeared in the <u>St. Paul Pioneer Press</u> of April 15, 1894, and in the <u>St. Paul Globe</u> of August 17, 1902.

The Department of Public Works has, for many years, maintained a volume recording the street name changes in the city. This book, which is by no means complete, and not

always accurate, was copied as a W.P.A. project, and a
carbon typescript is cataloged in the Library of the
Minnesota Historical Society under St. Paul Department of
Public Works: Guide to St. Paul Street Names before 1937.

An earlier and very useful guide to street name changes
occurs in Everett S. Geer's New Guide for citizens and
strangers to the location and numbers of streets and
avenues in the city of St. Paul.... published in St. Paul
by Everett S. Geer in 1884.

attempts to change the street names to a more logical system

Over the years, many residents and an even greater number
of visitors, have grumbled and complained about the lack
of system in the street names of St. Paul. "Surely," they
have argued, "it would be better to number all the streets,
or alphabetize them, or both. Anything," they insist,
"would be more comprehensible than the present hodgepodge
of individual names." These same disgruntled people will
then gesture significantly toward Minneapolis, and exclaim
that even they have a better system.

ODE TO THE STREET SYSTEM OF
SOUTHWEST MINNEAPOLIS
By Garrison Keillor

When you are beset by doubt,
Take Lyndale Avenue due south
Where you can put your mind at rest,
Knowing all streets run east and west
And all are perfectly numbered.
(There is, of course, no Twenty-third.
It was logically omitted to make
Thirtieth come out as Lake
Instead of an odd Thirty-first or -second.)
For years, successful men have reckoned
By this system, trained the self
To follow Lyndale and hang a ralph
At Fiftieth, into a neighborhood
Where homes are stable, children good,
Earnings are high and soundly invested
In products Consumer Reports has tested,
Where life is not paranoid, moody or radical,
But Republican, Lutheran and Alphabetical.

Aldrich, Bryant, Colfax, Dupont:
You can put your trust upon't
When hopes are few and times are hard—
Emerson, Fremont and Girard.
Humboldt, Irving, James and Knox:
This our foundation, these our bedrocks.
While Logan, Morgan, Newton, Oliver and Penn
Justify the ways of man to men,
There is order in the promise
Of Queen, Russell, Sheridan, Thomas.
O do not stop or make a turn
At Upton, Vincent or Washburn,
Knowing by then the system meaneth,
Past Xerxes, York, we'll reach our Zenith.

Be thankful this is not St. Paul.
There is no sense to it at all.
Where the Church, for all its spiritual and temporal powers,
Permits a jungle of streets named after trees and flowers.
Where a Minneapolis person can only look up to the heavens
As, driving on Eighth Street, he finds himself on Ninth and
    then on Seventh.

Reprinted, by permission, from
The Minneapolis Tribune,
January 20, 1974.

While there have been sporadic attempts to change the street naming system in St. Paul, only one concerted effort has been made. In August of 1907, Postmaster Edward Yanish proposed to the Commercial Club that St. Paul adopt the Philadelphia plan of naming and numbering streets. According to Yanish, Rice Street, Wabasha Street, Summit Avenue, and Hudson Avenue would divide the city into quadrants, each of which would have its own numbered sequence of streets. The West Side, with just twenty-six streets, would be arranged alphabetically.

By the following March, the City Council had appointed a committee to investigate changing the street name system. The local representative of the R. L. Polk Company, publisher of the city directory, proclaimed that St. Paul was as chaotic as Boston, and the sooner a new plan was adopted, the better off the city would be.

A month later, there were rumblings of protest, and an editorial in the St. Paul Pioneer Press ventured the opinion that:

> *In view of the fact that streets are named not*
> *for the purpose of embalming the memory of*
> *departed real estate dealers and their children,*
> *or of demonstrating their poetic fancy, but to*
> *serve as indices of the location of homes and*
> *business houses, and in view of the further fact*
> *that under any plan suggested there is room for*
> *the presentation of all important names of local*
> *flavor and significance, the Pioneer Press is at*
> *present inclined to think that the practical*
> *advantages to be gained by any reasonably simple*
> *and systematic plan far outweigh the sentimental*
> *and practical objections that have been raised.*

Now the battle lines were drawn.

A letter to the Editor signed by "A conservative" queried "who wants to be located by a vulgar fraction?" and reminded the readers of Longfellow who said: "We cannot buy with gold the old associations." In July, an article appeared in the St. Paul Dispatch proclaiming the women of the city against any change. In ending, the article declared:

> *No, the women are dead against it; they think*
> *St. Paul would lose its distinctiveness, and*
> *they believe that it would be to dishonor the*
> *men who struggled to make it what it is, to*
> *obliterate the old names and give us numbers*
> *as if we were in a penitentiary. So there,*
> *Mr. Postmaster, you know how we feel about it.*

In December of 1908, the women prepared a petition containing hundreds of signatures protesting any change in the system of street names. Besides the sentiment involved, the ladies also claimed the peculiar topography of certain parts of the city prevented any regular arrangement of the street names.

In March of 1909, a year and a half after the new system was first proposed, the committee appointed by the City Council was still meeting, but at this date they found it expedient to invite the women to meet with them.

By September the committee was prepared to submit its recommendations to the City Council for action. Miffed by the continuing opposition from so many prominent women in the city, the committee members, with male arrogance, ventured their opinion that if only the women thoroughly understood the new system, they would certainly favor it.

In December, the committee was still refining a master plan which by now included a number of personal names that would

also serve as numerical streets, in the way which Lake
Street in Minneapolis also serves as Thirtieth Street.

In the summer of 1911, the proposed street name system
finally came before the City Council where it was promptly
referred to the Committee on Streets who waited to act
until all voices had been heard.

In October of that same year, while the proposed ordinance
was still in Council committee, several of the aldermen
expressed their feelings that popular sentiment was opposed
to any change. The aldermen further asserted that while
one of the objects in adopting the ordinance would be to
facilitate the delivery of mail in St. Paul, the Post Office
had recently cut back its service, and consequently districts
of the city formerly having two or three deliveries a day,
were now receiving only one delivery. Thus, the aldermen
concluded, if the Post Office has retrenched on their service, the city will not gain anything by changing the names
of the streets to expedite delivery of the mail.

There the matter ended.

sources of information

With a few notable exceptions, there is no record, official
or otherwise, of why a street name was selected. It is
almost always necessary, therefore, to determine or infer
the significance of any name from the shreds of evidence
that can be gathered.

Any serious research must begin with the original plat on
file in the Register of Deeds office in the county court-
house. The plat must be examined for the original sequence
of street names, many of which may have since been changed.
The name of the developer should be determined, as well as
the names of the surveyor, notary public, or any other
individuals associated with the plat.

If none of these individuals seem related to the street
name, and subsequent biographical research cannot make any
connection, then a check of the ownership of the property
prior to the platting will often prove successful. In the
case of more recent plats, a telephone call to the developer
will usually ascertain the meaning of his street names.

If the plat does not provide a useful clue, then the research must be extended. Early atlases, maps, probate and district court records, city directories, genealogical data, newspapers, census records, histories of the city, manuscripts, periodicals, and, depending upon the name, a variety of other usual and unusual reference sources, will often supply the missing information.

Street name changes are always recorded in the City Council minutes. Because these changes are the result of a bureaucracy, it is very difficult to even guess why a certain name was chosen, and, as a class, these names present an often impossible problem.

Sometimes, however, the street names simply have no significance. They were chosen because they sounded nice, or seemed to have some promotional value. This is particularly true if the developer is a large company, a corporate entity, or a large-scale developer who, like the parent with twelve children, has become oblivious to the delight of bestowing a name.

Making a new street in St. Paul, Minnesota. (From "Harper's Weekly," October 25, 1890)

A STREET: The original sequence of streets, named in 1856, ran from A through K, but only A, B, and C remain. This was the first of several attempts at an alphabetical series of street names.

ABELL STREET: William and Mary Abell were among the developers of this land in 1882. He was a railroad clerk who lived in St. Paul from 1881-1883.

ACKER STREET: Captain William H. Acker (1833-1862), a bookkeeper by profession, was the Adjutant General of Minnesota in 1860-61. He was killed in the Civil War battle of Shiloh. The street was named in 1870 by his brother-in-law, Edmund Rice, the developer of the area.

ADA STREET: Previously Washington Street, the name was changed in 1876. Many streets in St. Paul bear women's first names.

ADOLPHUS STREET: This street was named in 1871, probably for some member of the family of Robert Smith or William Dawson, the developers. Other streets were named Emma, Louise, Mary, Larry, Agnes, and Tina.

ADRIAN STREET: This was most likely a personal name when the street was platted in 1881.

AGATE STREET: Acknowledging the fine grained rock which is now the state gemstone, this street was named in 1870 by Edmund Rice. An intersecting street is called Granite.

AGNES AVENUE: Edmund and Agnes Wilgus dabbled in real estate, platting this street in 1886. They resided in St. Paul about thirteen years before moving to New York City in 1893.

AIDA PLACE: The other avenues within Como Park were officially named, in 1967, for past park managers. This street, however, was named for Aida, the mother of Victor Tedesco. A long-time City Council member, he was at that

time Park Commissioner. Antonio Drive in Highland Park is
named for his father.

ALABAMA STREET: Platted as Second Street, the name was
changed in 1876 to correspond with the adjacent streets
which were also named for states.

ALAMEDA STREET: Previously Langtry Street, the name was
changed in 1940, as part of a general reorganization of
street names. Alameda is Spanish and indicates a park or
grove of trees. There are several places with this name,
most notably a city and county in California.

ALASKA AVENUE: This street was named in 1886 for the then
territory of Alaska where gold was discovered that same
year, making the name a popular and appealing one.

ALBANY AVENUE: Originally named Villard Avenue, the name
was changed in 1886 to avoid duplication. Albany is a
short name, easy to spell and pronounce.

ALBEMARLE STREET: Applied to this street in 1857, Albemarle
is a county in Virginia which took its name from an early
governor of that state.

ALBERT STREET: John Wann, an Englishman and early landowner
and developer in the Summit Hill area, named this street in
1874 for Prince Albert (1819-1861), husband of Queen
Victoria of England.

ALBION AVENUE: In 1881 this name was in vogue; it comes
from the mythological name for England.

ALCOVE STREET: Previously Chestnut Street, the name was
changed in 1886 to avoid duplication. Alcove can mean a
"recess among trees or vines" which seems appropriate for
a small street.

ALDINE STREET: Platted as Wright Street, the name was
changed in 1886. This is an unusual name that may refer
to the Aldine Press which published editions of classics
in the early years of printing, and by extension, sometimes refers to finely printed books. The name has a nice
sound and pleasant associations, but it hardly seems
appropriate. It is, however, almost unknown as a personal
or place name.

ALGONQUIN AVENUE: One of several Indian names in the 1917
addition of Beaver Lake Heights, this one specifies a group
of Indian tribes.

ALICE STREET: Both the street and park were named in 1879
for Alice, daughter of William Dawson (1825-1901) who
developed the area. He was at one time the Mayor of St.
Paul, a banker, and a leading land speculator, but his

Bank of Minnesota failed in 1896, and Dawson died a poor man.

ALLSTON STREET: Allston is an area within the city of Boston, on the right bank of the Charles River. The name was chosen by the Union Land Company in 1887 for its appealing sound.

ALMOND AVENUE: Originally Orange Street, the name was changed in 1886 to avoid duplication. Many of the street names were changed at this time; very few of the newer ones had any particular significance.

ALTAMONT STREET: This is a synthetic name popular in the nineteenth century. Alta is Italian, meaning high; mont is French, meaning mountain. The exotic sound made it a popular choice in 1888.

ALTON STREET: Alton is a city in Illinois best known locally as the home of Robert Smith who gave Smith Park (now Mears Park) to the city. This street was named in 1872 by another Illinois developer, Charles Weide.

AMES AVENUE: This street was named in 1886 for William Leonard Ames (1846-1910) and his wife, Helen (1854-1940), the developers of Hazel Park. William, born in New Jersey, journeyed with his father of the same name to St. Paul in 1850. His father purchased land in and about the city, including a three-hundred acre stock farm where he raised nationally known shorthorn cattle in the area today bounded by Hazelwood, Arlington, Case, and White Bear avenues.
    William, Jr. attended the Naval Academy at Annapolis and later worked at the cattle business in the West, returning to St. Paul upon his father's death in 1873. By this time, the family owned 1200 acres southeast of Lake Phalen, which he platted into Hazel Park and other real estate subdivisions. The Ames School is named for him. William's home, built about 1890, still stands at 1667 Ames Avenue.

AMES PLACE: Originally part of Stillwater Avenue, this segment was renamed in 1940.

AMHERST STREET: Like the other streets within Macalester Park, this one was named in 1883 for a college; in this case, Amherst College in Amherst, Massachusetts. Other streets similarly named were Princeton, Cambridge, Oxford, Rutgers, Dartmouth, and Macalester.

ANDREW STREET: Platted as Jackson Street, the name was changed in 1876. Many streets were renamed to avoid duplication when West St. Paul (now the West Side) was annexed to St. Paul which already had a Jackson Street.

ANITA STREET: The West Side Land and Cottage Company named
this street in 1883. The use of feminine names was a common
practice then, as now.

ANN STREET: James M. Winslow platted this street in 1851.
Because an adjacent street was named Blair, perhaps Ann
represents the wife of John Blair, a nationally known
capitalist and political figure who was active in railroad
promotion.

ANN ARBOR: Ann is one of the commonest women's names which,
because of its brevity, is often combined with another word.
The name was, in 1890, most likely chosen both for its
euphony, and for the city of the same name in Michigan.

*Looking east on Annapolis Street from Robert Street in the 1920's.
The houses in the background remain, but the grocery store, once
a saloon, has been replaced. The streetcar is turning around for
another trip downtown.*

ANNAPOLIS STREET: Originally named 13th Street in one
section, and Cottage Street in another, these names were
changed in 1876. With the annexation of West St. Paul
(now the West Side) by St. Paul, this street became the
southern boundary of St. Paul and the dividing line between
Ramsey and Dakota Counties. The name is most likely from
the capital city of Maryland.

ANTONIO DRIVE: This was named as one of the streets within Highland Park by the St. Paul City Council in 1967. Antonio is the father of Victor Tedesco, long-time City Council member, and at the time, Park Commissioner. Aida Place in Como Park is named for Tedesco's mother.

ARBOR STREET: Platted as Third Street, the name was changed in 1872 to avoid duplication with another Third Street (now Kellogg Boulevard). Arbor signifies trees or a shady garden spot.

ARCADE STREET: According to the dictionary, an arcade is "an arched or covered passageway or avenue, specifically one between rows of shops." This street, named in 1872 by Bernard Sinnen, was of course wishful thinking since nothing existed there except a survey line on a map.

ARCH STREET: On the 1856 plat, this street forms an arch on the top of the page which is still discernible on a street map of today.

ARGYLE STREET: Argyle is a county in Scotland which gives title to the Campbell family; in other words, members of the Campbell family are the Dukes, Earls, and Marquesses of Argyle. Among the developers of this street in 1885 were Henry and Minnesota Campbell.

ARKWRIGHT STREET: Sir Richard Arkwright (1732-1792) was the first manufacturer of cotton cloth, and an important figure in the textile industry. The developer of this area in 1853 was from New York state, near the village of Arkwright, and familiar with the textile industry.

ARLINGTON AVENUE: Previously the Lake Como-Phalen Road, the name was changed in 1940. It was originally a county road between Lakes Como and Phalen and also the north boundary of the city in the 1880's. For a few years around 1885, John Morgan and Joseph H. Williams had an iron rolling mill in a large brick building on the north side of Arlington, at Woodbridge Street. This name change was part of a general reorganization and was prompted by the Arlington Hills addition, made some eighty years earlier near the eastern edge of this street. The first name, however, was more historic, descriptive, and exact.

ARMSTRONG AVENUE: Born in Ohio, George W. Armstrong (1827-1917) traveled to St. Paul by way of Keokuk, Iowa. He was State Treasurer from 1857 to 1860; afterwards he dealt in real estate, naming this street in 1873. Armstrong believed the easiest and best way to make money was to put it out for interest, "for interest goes on when you sleep, when you wake, when you weep, when you rejoice, when you die."

ARONA STREET: Arona is a town in northern Italy about thirty miles west of Como; this proximity suggested the name in 1885.

ARUNDEL STREET: In 1855 Charles Mackubin named this street for Anne Arundel County in Maryland, his native state.

ASBURY STREET: Autocratic and domineering, a man of resolute will, Francis Asbury (1745-1816) was a prime organizer and driving force in the Methodist Episcopal Church of America. The street was named for him in 1881 because of its proximity to Hamline University, which had a Methodist Episcopal affiliation.

ASHLAND AVENUE: This is a name chosen in 1870, like the two adjacent streets, Laurel and Holly, for its favorable connotations and general euphony. It has no literal meaning. Ashland was also the name of Henry Clay's estate which contributed to the popularity of the name.

ATLANTIC STREET: Platted as Collins Street, the name was changed in 1874. An adjacent street termed Ocean most likely prompted the new name.

ATTY STREET: Named in 1885, this is either a personal name, or the abbreviation for attorney.

ATWATER STREET: Originally Pleasant Street, the name was changed in 1872, probably in honor of Edward D. Atwater, secretary of the land department of the St. Paul and Pacific Railway. There is also a village in Kandiyohi County named for him. Atwater, a civil engineer by profession, was born in Vermont about 1834, and departed St. Paul in 1879.

AUDITORIUM STREET: First named Franklin Street in 1849 (for Benjamin Franklin), this name was changed in 1940 to avoid conflict with Franklin Avenue. Auditorium refers to the St. Paul Auditorium opened in April, 1907. Promoted by Edmund W. Bazille, designed by architect Allen H. Stem, built at a cost of $435,000, with a capacity of up to 10,500 people, this was to be the showplace of St. Paul. The newspapers were lavish in their praise of the swinging balconies, the twenty-two boxes in the theatre, the hanging lamps, the frescoed foyers, and the fireproof construction.

AURORA AVENUE: A popular noun of the nineteenth century, Aurora means literally the rising light of the morning, the dawn of the day. It was applied to this street in 1857.

AVON STREET: Originally Cayuga Street, the name was changed in 1872 to signify the historic river of England with Shakespearian associations.

B

B STREET: The original sequence of streets, named in 1856, ran from A through K. Only A, B, and C remain. This was the first attempt at an alphabetical series of street names.

BAILEY STREET: John Vincent Bailey (1872-1943) operated a nursery in the area when this street was named in 1926. His grandchildren now manage the business.

BAKER STREET: Daniel A. J. Baker (1825-1909) was a developer of this area in 1857. Baker was born in Maine and arrived in St. Paul in 1849 where he taught one of the first public schools in the Territory. He afterwards practiced law, and was among the founders of Superior, Wisconsin. Just after the Civil War, he acquired 160 acres in what was then Rose Township, and built a house near the intersection of Pelham Boulevard and Wabash Avenue. The Baker School stands on land he donated near the northeast boundary of his farm.
     There is a humorous anecdote recorded about Baker, who in trying to save his barn from his creditors, had it moved into the middle of the public street on a Sunday when legal papers preventing him could not be served. He later argued that the men moving the barn were under the influence of liquor, and could not be blamed for their actions, thus, logically, if no one were responsible, the barn must have moved itself.

BALSAM STREET: This street was named in 1946. Tree names are always popular.

BANCROFT AVENUE: Platted as Cambridge Street, the name was changed in 1886. Bancroft is a common name, and most likely no one individual was indicated, but there might have been a passing thought for George Bancroft (1800-1891), American politician and historian.

BANFIL STREET: Considered "a man of sterling worth," John Banfil (1812?-1887) was a native of New York, and subsequently a resident of New Orleans. He moved to Prairie du Chien in 1840, then to St. Paul in 1846, where he platted

this street in 1851. He later moved to Manomin (now
Fridley) where he built a sawmill on Rice Creek, and from
there to Bayfield, Wisconsin, in 1866.

BARCLAY STREET: Previously Moore Street, the name was
changed in 1886. Barclay is a common personal and place
name, with the additional advantage of being easy to pronounce and spell.

BARRETT STREET: Frank and Carrie Crowell developed Crowell
and Barrett streets in 1907. John W. Barrett was vice-
president of the Western Land Company.

BARTLETT COURT: This street was named in 1885 for John M.
Bartlett (1830-1922) of the Minneapolis real estate firm
of Bartlett and Marsh. He had a financial interest in the
St. Anthony Park Company.

BASSWOOD AVENUE: For those who don't like people dropping
in on them, this is the address. One of St. Paul's "ghost
streets," the only present access is from South St. Paul
across the Mississippi River. This street was part of
Riverside Park, platted in 1889 along the old territorial
road to Point Douglas. The community was never large, but
it persisted for years until finally obliterated by the
1965 flood. The Park contained some very early log cabins
built by the French voyageurs who lived there in the
earliest days of St. Paul.

BATAVIA STREET: Previously Beacon Street, the name was
changed to avoid duplication in 1940. Batavia is a name
generally applied to the Netherlands, and by extension to
the Dutch immigrant settlements. It is a common place name.

BATES AVENUE: Maria Bates Dayton, the daughter of Master
Bates, was a native of Providence, Rhode Island where she
was born about 1811. The wife of Lyman Dayton, a successful
real estate speculator, she moved to Dayton in Hennepin
County upon his death in 1865. This street, and Maria
Avenue, were named for her in 1857.

BATTLE CREEK ROAD: Platted as part of Hazel Avenue, the
name was changed at the request of the residents in 1957.
The change was desirable because of the large gap between
this street and the remainder of Hazel Avenue.

BAY STREET: This street was named in 1856 for the Bay tree,
better known as a Laurel tree.

BAYARD AVENUE: Frederick L. Bayard was a local real estate
man just setting up in business when this street was named
in 1886. Born in New York, he settled in St. Paul about
1882. He died in 1927 at age seventy-five, having dealt in
St. Paul real estate for close to forty-five years. The
family pronounces the name Bye-erd. The well known street

MARIA BATES DAYTON
"her barque, lighted by the love and charity she has given to others here on earth, will guide her safely to the dim unknown"

of the same name in New York City is named for distant ancestors of this family.

BAYFIELD STREET: Originally 4th Street, the name was changed in 1883. This is a common place name.

BAYLESS AVENUE: Vincent W. Bayless, a Minneapolis resident, was president of the St. Anthony Park Company which was incorporated in 1885. Before moving to Dubuque, Iowa in 1926, he also dealt in timber lands, investments, and fuel.

BEACON AVENUE: Named in 1886, this is part of Howard Park. The name is uncertain; my best guess is that it remembers Beacon Street in Boston, part of an exclusive residential district.

BEAUMONT STREET: Platted as Vine Street, the name was changed in 1872 in honor of Joseph I. Beaumont (1827-1905). He migrated to St. Paul in 1855, was a member of the City Council, chief fire warden of the city, and later, Ramsey County Assessor. He was generally liked, and known as a quiet, pleasant gentleman.

BEAVER STREET: Originally Douglas Street, the name was changed to avoid duplication, in 1886.

BEDFORD STREET: Previously Main Street, the name was changed in 1872. There are a number of places with this name; probably all stem from the county and town in England.

BEECH STREET: A reference to the tree, Beech Street was
platted in 1857 as Franklin Street. The name was changed
in 1872 to avoid conflict with Franklin Street downtown.

BEECHWOOD AVENUE: Named in 1925 by the Highland Park
Company, this is one of many, many streets within the city
using the names of trees.

BELLOWS STREET: At first unnamed, this was designated
Bellows Street in 1876. Many of these streets were renamed
when the West Side was annexed to St. Paul. This is probably a personal name, but whose I cannot say.

BELVIDERE STREET: Originally Martha Street, the name was
changed in 1883. Belvidere is Italian for "beautiful view;"
it is quite a common name.

BENA STREET: Bena is said to be a Chippewa word, meaning
partridge. It was applied in 1917 as part of Beaver Lake
Heights.

BENHILL ROAD: Platted as Ridgewood Avenue, the name was
changed in 1915. Ben is a Gaelic/Irish term meaning a
mountain or hill. It was most likely selected because it
has a more distinguished sound.

BENSON AVENUE: George and Emma Benson of Wabasha County,
Minnesota were the developers of this street in 1884.

BERKELEY AVENUE: Previously named Lydia Street, the name
was changed in 1913. This was done, no doubt, at the wish
of the developer of Macalester Villas who wanted his street
names to identify with those inside Macalester Park.
Berkeley refers to the University of California at Berkeley,
California. Stanford and Wellesley avenues, also representing colleges, derive their names from the same source. This
is the second Berkeley Street within the area; for a time
Palace Avenue was also named Berkeley.

BERLAND PLACE: Isaac Berland, his son Morton, and their
wives, Ethel and Shirley developed this area in 1960.
Building contractors under the name Cardinal Construction
Company, they laid out the streets which were named for an
alphabetical sequence: Afton Road, Berland, Cardinal,
Dellridge, Edgebrook, Falcon, Glenridge, Hillsdale, Kipling,
Longfellow, Morningside. The names are largely without
further significance.

BERRY STREET: Either the fruit, or an individual, or a
fruity individual prompted this name in 1886.

BEULAH LANE: Born in Kansas City, Missouri, a graduate of
Villa Marie Academy in Frontenac, Beulah Bartlett (1890-1969)
served as Executive Director of the St. Paul Humane Society

from 1923 to 1963. When the new Humane Society headquarters was built at its present location in 1954, the street leading to it was named in her honor.

BEVERLY ROAD: The Union Land Company named this street in 1887 for the city and summer resort on an inlet of the Atlantic Ocean, near Boston.

BIDWELL STREET: Ira Bidwell (1804?-1876?) was one of the investors in West Side land when this street was named about 1855. A native of Vermont, Bidwell came to St. Paul from Wisconsin about 1854. He opened Bidwell's Exchange Bank, but later devoted himself exclusively to real estate. He had two sons, Albert and Henry, both of whom farmed on the West Side. The original Bidwell Street was one block west of its present location.

BIGELOW AVENUE: This development was platted in 1918 as the Midway Industrial Division by Herbert H. Bigelow, of Brown and Bigelow, Gebhard Bohn of the Bohn Refrigerator Company, and Eli S. Warner, of McGill-Warner Corporation. The area, known as Kittsondale, was formerly the horse stables and farms of Norman Kittson, reputedly the richest man in the Northwest. Herbert H. Bigelow (1870-1933) was born near Brookfield, Vermont. At age thirteen, with his family, he moved to Iowa, and subsequently graduated from Grinnell College, after which he worked as a calendar salesman. In 1896, he joined with Hiram D. Brown, a printer, to form Brown and Bigelow, a firm printing and selling advertising calendars. In 1907, Bigelow made his first purchase of Midway property, and the present office building on University Avenue was completed in 1914. Under his management, the firm grew to be the largest of its kind in the world. Mr. Bigelow died under questionable circumstances in September of 1933.

BIGLOW LANE: This street was added to the city in 1950 as part of the McDonough public housing project. Robert Biglow (1922-1943) was a Seaman 2nd Class who was missing in action after the sinking of the destroyer, U.S.S. DeHaven off Guadalcanal during World War II. His name was suggested by a veterans' organization. John J. McDonough (1895-1962) for whom the project was named, was Mayor of St. Paul from 1940-48.

BIRCH STREET: This street was named in 1926, most likely for the tree.

BIRCH VIEW COURT: The street overlooked a clump of birch when it was named in 1965.

BIRMINGHAM STREET: Thomas F. Birmingham (1848-1932), his wife, Mary, and his brother, William platted this street in 1884. Birmingham journeyed to St. Paul in 1857 with his parents. He worked at several occupations while dabbling in real estate. In 1884 he and his brother were running a grocery store.

BISON AVENUE: This street was named in 1913 by Thomas Frankson, for his herd of bison (American buffalo). He purchased the buffalo in Iowa and had them brought to his zoo in Spring Valley, Minnesota where he lived. He subsequently transported them to St. Paul where he had them in an enclosure between Bison Avenue and Midway Parkway.

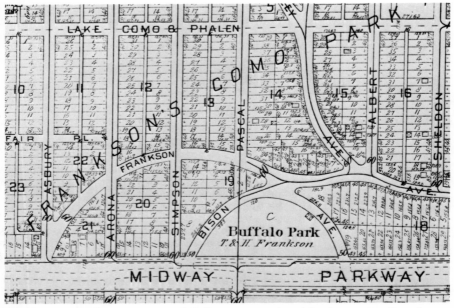

A gimmick attracting potential buyers to view his lots, Frankson's Buffalo Park gave the adjacent Bison Avenue its name.

BLAIR AVENUE: This street was quite possibly named for Francis Preston Blair (1821-1875) and his father of the same name (1791-1876). Both journalists and politicians, they advocated development of the West, cheap lands for settlers, and other policies, endearing themselves to the frontier Midwest. Both campaigned for Lincoln and were anti-slavery. The younger Blair actively campaigned for the Republican cause in Minnesota. This street was named in 1872.

BLAKE AVENUE: Anson Blake, his nephew, Charles H. Pratt, and William R. Marshall, were principal owners and agents of the south part of St. Anthony Park, platted in 1885. All three were incorporators of the St. Anthony Park

Company, and Blake served for a time as secretary and treasurer. He died May 6, 1906, at the age of eighty-seven.

BOHLAND AVENUE: Adam Bohland owned a farm of eighty acres between Cleveland, Fairview, Montreal, and Bohland avenues. Adam (1834-1913) was born in Sulzheim, Germany, and came to Minnesota in 1856. He fought in the Civil War, served as County Commissioner and was later County Assessor. Adam's brother, Peter Bohland (1837-1910), owned the remaining quarter section: eighty acres between Cleveland, Fairview, Montreal, and Magoffin avenues. The houses of the two brothers faced each other across Montreal Avenue about where Prior Avenue would cross. This street was named in 1887.

BOLSER STREET: Named in 1926 as part of the Bachman Addition, this is most likely a personal name, but whose I do not know.

BORDNER PLACE: Kenneth Bordner, a real estate man, purchased this tax-forfeited property from the city in 1946. Since 1950, Bordner has worked nationally as a land use consultant.

BOURNE AVENUE: Walter B. Bourne, a clerk for the sale of lots, notarized this plat in 1885. He lived in St. Paul until his death on October 10, 1916, at age fifty-seven. He was buried in Red Wing.

BOWDOIN STREET: The streets in this area (Hiawatha Park) were originally named, in 1890, for colleges: Colgate, Cornell, Yale, and Colby. Bowdoin College in Maine was attended by Longfellow, who later taught there.

BOXWOOD AVENUE: Platted in 1889 as part of Riverside Park along the river, this street has been extended to the north along the top of the bluff. Other street names in Riverside Park were Blackwood, Redwood, Whitewood, Basswood, etc., all of which are "ghost streets" today.

BRADFORD STREET: William Bradford (1590-1657) was one of the Pilgrim fathers who served as governor of the Plymouth colony. He is remembered by this street named in 1885 as part of St. Anthony Park.

BRADLEY STREET: Newton Bradley was a merchant who lived at Broadway and Sixth; Joshua Bradley was a Baptist clergyman who died in St. Paul in 1855. Either may have served as the namesake of this street platted in 1852.

BRAINERD AVENUE: In 1867, two years after the Civil War, a road meandered north out of St. Paul, following roughly the course of Highway 35E today. At Maryland Avenue, the road swung northeast and came up the hill in a natural ravine,

from whence it followed exactly the course of Brainerd
Avenue to Edgerton Avenue. This New Canada Township road
then swung north to Little Canada. The early date accounts
for the diagonal course of the street.

Horace J. Brainerd and his family had, in 1867, a
twenty-three acre farm in the area today enclosed by Ivy,
Payne, Clear, Greenbrier, Sherwood, and Edgerton streets.
Brainerd (1825-1902), a native of Cleveland, Ohio, moved
to New Lisbon, Wisconsin with his family at the age of
sixteen. In 1849 he married and came to Ramsey County in
1851, purchasing his farm three years later. He was very
active in the affairs of the township, serving as a state
legislator, and Ramsey County Commissioner. The street,
which bypassed his farm, was officially named in 1886.

BRANSTON STREET: The English village in Lincolnshire
provided this name in 1885. British names are always a
fertile source of inspiration.

BREDA AVENUE: Originally platted west of Fairview Avenue
in 1885 as part of St. Anthony Park, the street was extended
east, while the western part was vacated. Breda is a town
in the Netherlands, where the peace between England and
Holland was signed in 1667.

BREEN AVENUE: Frederick L. Breen was chief deputy register
of deeds for Ramsey County from 1896 to 1934. This street
was named in 1928.

BREWSTER STREET: Previously Alden Street and Alden Place,
the name was changed in 1940. William Brewster (1567-1644)
was an elder of the Pilgrim Church, who came to America on
the Mayflower.

BRIGHTON PLACE: Brighton was the principal seaside resort
of England, with many elegant streets, squares, terraces,
and fine parks. It was a most fashionable resort when this
name was transferred to the shores of Lake Phalen in 1886.

BRIMHALL STREET: William Brimhall (1825-1897) was born in
Hardwick, Massachusetts. At the age of ten he began working
on a neighboring farm; eight years later he was apprenticed
to the plowmaker's trade. He subsequently worked as a
carpenter, almost losing his life when a dam he helped con-
struct across the Connecticut River gave way. He came to
Minnesota in 1851, boarding with his uncle, Lot Moffett, a
well known pioneer. Taking a claim of eighty acres in an
area today bounded by St. Clair, Randolph, Pascal, and
Snelling avenues, Brimhall experimented with the raising of
fruits and vegetables, planting twenty-five acres of apple
trees. He was also proprietor of the Reserve Nursery and a
lifelong member of the State Horticultural Society. In 1886,
"having outlived the climate," he platted his farm into
building lots and moved to San Diego, California.

BROADWAY: A common street name, although probably best known in New York City, this was one of the first streets in St. Paul platted in 1849.

BROMPTON STREET: Brompton was a district of London, England when this street was named in 1885.

BROOKLINE STREET: Brookline is a village near Boston, noted for its elegant villas, beautiful gardens and parks. The name was applied to this street in 1887 by the Union Land Company.

BROWN AVENUE: William Reynolds Brown (1816-1874) named this street in 1857. Born near Urbana, Ohio, he moved to Wabash County, Illinois in 1833 where he became a journey-man carpenter. In 1841, with the promise of a year's work and good wages, he accompanied a Methodist missionary via St. Louis to Red Rock, being the first white settler on that prairie. He farmed there until 1852 when he moved to West St. Paul where he purchased and platted some property. In 1857, he considered himself worth $50,000; the crash that same year reduced him to poverty. He lived for a time in St. Paul, served in the Civil War, and later re-turned to Newport where he died.

Reputed to be the first brick house in St. Paul, the Benjamin Brunson home remains at 485 Kenny Road. This photo was taken in November, 1896.

BRUNSON STREET: Originally a continuation of Burr Street, the name was changed in 1885 to honor Benjamin W. Brunson (1823-1898). Born in Detroit, he moved to St. Paul in 1847

where he assisted in surveying the original townsite.
Brunson was a member of the Territorial legislature, and a
leading citizen of the city for fifty years. He built, in
1855, what is reputed to be one of the first brick houses
in the city on the corner of Patridge (now Kenny Road) and
Brunson streets, where he lived until his death in 1898.
This home still stands at 485 Kenny Road, one of the oldest
houses in the city, and a direct link with the beginnings
of St. Paul.

BUFFALO STREET: Named in 1870 for the animal. An adjacent
street is called Elk.

BUFORD AVENUE: This street was named in 1885 in commemora-
tion of Abraham Buford (1820-1884). Member of a prominent
Virginia family, Buford was graduated from West Point and
participated in the war with Mexico. At the outbreak of
the Civil War he was appointed a Brigadier-General in the
Confederate Army. After the war he returned to his successful stock farm, but in later years, suffering the loss of
his son, wife, and home, he took his own life. His name
was selected for the street by the syndicate of Virginia
capitalists who provided financial backing for this plat.

BURG STREET: Leo J. Burg of Hennepin County was the mort-
gagee on this property when it was subdivided in 1926.

BURGESS STREET: Platted with no name, this street was
identified by the city in 1874, most likely for Clarence
Burgess, an engineer, and his sister, Louise M. Burgess,
a clerk, both of whom were working for the City Engineer's
office at this date. Louise subsequently worked with
David L. Curtice (surveyor, engineer, and map maker) for
many years.

BURLINGTON ROAD: The nearby Chicago, Burlington and Quincy
Railroad gave the name to this street--part of Burlington
Park--in 1886.

BURNQUIST STREET: Jacob A. A. Burnquist (1879-1961) was
Governor of Minnesota when this street was named in 1916.
Born in Dayton, Iowa, he graduated from Carleton College in
1902, and later the University of Minnesota Law School. He
was a state legislator from 1908-1912, Lieutenant Governor
from 1912-1915, Governor from 1915-1921, and Attorney
General from 1938-1954. In addition to his many political
honors and awards, he was also the author of a history of
Minnesota.

BURNS AVENUE: Benjamin Hoyt sold a $10,000 interest in the
1856 Suburban Hills plat to John Burns and his wife,
Priscilla. It does not appear the Burnses were ever residents of St. Paul.

BURR STREET: Benjamin Brunson named this street in 1852 to honor his mother, Eunice Burr. A native of Bridgeport, Connecticut, she came to Prairie du Chien with her missionary husband in 1836. She died there, from influenza, ten years later.

BUSH AVENUE: Originally named Fauquier Street in 1857 (for the county in Virginia), the name was changed one hundred years later to honor Archibald G. Bush (1887-1966), a chief executive of the 3M Company which for many years has had its offices on this street. Born and raised in Granite Falls, Minnesota, Bush joined 3M as assistant bookkeeper in 1909, early in the company's history. He was rapidly promoted to sales manager in 1914, a director of the company in 1921, executive vice-president in 1948, and chairman of the executive committee the following year. Bush, reputed to be one of the richest men in Minnesota, was an active philanthropist through the Bush Foundation.

BUTTERNUT AVENUE: Part of the Protestant Orphan Asylum property, this street name was selected in 1882 because there was a grove of butternut trees nearby.

C

C STREET: The original sequence of streets, named in 1856, ran from A through K. Only A, B, and C remain. This was the first attempt at an alphabetical series of street names.

CALIFORNIA AVENUE: Following the pattern set in Washington, D.C., this street was named in 1886 for the state. This area of the city includes only the western states. Hoyt Avenue was originally Kansas Avenue.

CAMBRIDGE STREET: Like the other streets within Macalester Park, this one was named in 1883 for a college; in this case, Cambridge University in England. Other streets were Princeton, Amherst, Cambridge, Oxford, Rutgers, Dartmouth, and Macalester.

CANFIELD STREET; CANFIELD AVENUE: This street within the Fairgrounds, and this avenue outside the Fairgrounds, honor Thomas H. Canfield (1875-1965), longtime secretary and general manager of the Minnesota Agricultural Society (State Fair). Born in Vermont, he came to Minnesota as a young man, where he operated a large stock farm near Detroit Lakes. From 1916 to 1930 he was with the Fair, later moving to Glendale, California, where he died.

CANTON STREET: This was a very popular place name, occurring in about twenty-five states, and having as its origin Canton, China. About the beginning of the nineteenth century the habit arose of giving foreign and strange sounding names to towns and villages, such as Memphis, Cairo, Hannibal. Such names were fashionable, stemming in part from a Post Office requirement that no name be duplicated within a state, and no street name be duplicated within a city. The name was applied to this street in 1874.

CAPITOL BOULEVARD: Originally Brewster Street, the name was changed in 1897 to reflect the proximity of the street to the State Capitol building then under construction. However, plans for making it part of a scenic boulevard between the Capitol and Como Park never materialized. See also Commonwealth Avenue.

CAPITOL HEIGHTS: Originally part of Jackson Street, the
name was changed in 1906 when Jackson was rerouted. The
name refers to the newly completed State Capitol.

CAPP ROAD: Originally railroad property used as a dump-
ing grounds, it was reclaimed and improved by Martin Capp,
who named the street in 1957. A Twin Cities developer
since 1946, Mr. Capp has been active in many phases of
construction.

CARDINAL PLACE: See Berland Place.

CARLETON STREET: I doubt this name, applied in 1881, has
any particular significance.

CARROLL AVENUE: Charles Carroll (1737-1832) of Maryland,
was a Revolutionary War leader and patriot. Upon his
death, he was the last surviving signer of the Declaration
of Independence, and the wealthiest citizen of the United
States. The developer of this street in 1855 was a native
of Maryland.

CARTER AVENUE: This plat was financed by a syndicate of
Virginia capitalists, among them: Hill Carter, James H.
Dooley, and Manley B. Curry, all of Richmond, Virginia.
Each had a street named for him.

CARVER AVENUE: First mapped as North Avenue, subsequently
changed to Polander Road (for the Polish farmers who lived
along it), this street assumed its present name in 1923.
Carver Lake, the ultimate destination of the street, takes
its name from Thomas Carver (1819-1883) who owned farm land
on all sides of the lake. Born in Glasgow, Scotland,
Thomas was a descendant of Jonathan Carver, the early
Minnesota explorer for whom Carver's Cave is named. Thomas
came to McLean Township as it was then known in 1852. The
family has remained in the immediate area for over one
hundred years, and has been active in the affairs of the
community. The present Carver School is named for the
family, and Carver was considered as a possible name for
the new suburb now known as Maplewood.

CASE AVENUE: Born in New York, James A. Case (1823-1896)
traveled to St. Paul in 1853, where he worked as a surveyor
and civil engineer. He was active in many early St. Paul
enterprises when this street was named in 1872.

CATHLIN STREET: Originally part of Prior Avenue, this
street was redeeded to the city in 1963 by the adjacent
railroad. The identity of Cathlin is not known.

CAYUGA STREET: Cayuga County in New York state gave this
street its name in 1870. That county derived its name
from the Cayuga Indian tribe, one of the six nations of the

JAMES A. CASE,

LAND AGENT,

CIVIL ENGINEER

AND

SURVEYOR.

Office on Saint Anthony Street,

OPPOSITE THE FIRST PRESBYTERIAN CH RCH,

ST. PAUL, MINNESOTA.

Iroquois League. Adjacent streets were called Seneca and Genesee which are also New York counties.

CECELIA PLACE: This street was added to the city in 1886 by Herman Haupt, Jr., a patent attorney, whose father was General Manager of the Northern Pacific Railroad. Cecelia is a personal name, but whose I cannot say.

CEDAR STREET: Named in 1849, this is one of the first streets of St. Paul. It was so called because of the red cedar trees on the Mississippi bluff at the river end of the street.

CENTRAL AVENUE: Part of the plat containing Central Park, this street was named in 1884. Today the park is the site of a state parking ramp, but a portion of the street, with its center boulevard, remains.

CHAMBER STREET: Previously Oxford Avenue, the name was changed to avoid duplication in 1940. Other street names in the vicinity were Harvard, Yale, and Vassar. The significance of this new name, if any, is not apparent.

CHAMBERS STREET: There are two members of the Chambers
family--father and son--who seem equally worthy of this
street name within the Fairgrounds. Alexander Chambers
was born in New York and moved to Minnesota in 1859. Like
many of the pioneers, he was very interested in agriculture
and served as President of the Minnesota State Agricultural
Society in 1868. His son, Clarke A. Chambers (1839-1919)
helped run the affairs of the Society as a Manager from
1882 until 1897. This street was at first named Simpson
for an early Secretary of the Society, but the name was
changed at the request of Clarke Chambers' widow.

CHANNEL STREET: First mapped as Ninth Street, the name was
changed in 1883 in reference to a creek that began near
Holman Field, flowed along the railroad tracks, and then
along the course of Channel Street to Water Street. After
meandering west along Water Street for a half-mile or so,
the stream dropped into the river.
      Once the site of Castle Royal, an extravagant night-
club hollowed into the cliff at Wabasha and Channel, the
street now, unmarked and barely discernible, runs along the
base of the cliffs for a couple of blocks, then turns right
to intersect Plato Boulevard.

CHARLES AVENUE: A brother of Edmund Rice, the developer,
Charles Rodney Rice (1821-1873) was a merchant here for a
short time, but later moved to Washington, D.C. The street
was named in 1854.

CHARLOTTE STREET: Charlotte Taylor, with her husband,
William, purchased this property in 1873, platted it in
1882, and sold it in 1887. They were not local residents.

CHARLTON STREET: Charlton, Massachusetts was the birthplace
of Dwight Woodbury, one of the investors in West Side real
estate.

CHATSWORTH STREET: "Chatsworth House," the home of the Duke
of Devonshire, was one of the most magnificent private
residences in England when this street was named in 1871.
The developer, John Wann (1829-1905) was born in Belfast,
Ireland, and worked for the East India Company before
migrating to St. Paul in 1865. Wann's large mansion stood
on the corner of Victoria and Summit·avenues where Our Lady
of Peace High School now stands. He sold this home to
Archbishop Ireland who planned on building a great St. Paul-
Minneapolis Cathedral on this neutral midway site.

CHELMSFORD STREET: Chelmsford was a municipal borough of
England, and capital of Essex County in 1885 when this
street was named.

CHELSEA STREET: This street was named as part of Chelsea
Heights in 1916. Chelsea is a suburban quarter of London
on the north bank of the Thames River.

Chelsea Heights was the remainder of the Joshua Robertson (1822-1913) farm. Robertson married the sister of Auguste L. Larpenteur; after their marriage they moved to St. Paul in 1852. Two years later Robertson bought eighty acres between Snelling and Hamline, Arlington and Larpenteur avenues; he later expanded his farm northeast. The Robertson farm house once stood on what is today the northeast corner of Arlington and Hamline avenues.

CHELTON AVENUE: This street name was derived in 1885 from Chelten Hills, then a railroad station a few miles north of Philadelphia where Hannah Tatum, one of the investors, lived.

CHEROKEE AVENUE: The Park and the Boulevard take their name from this street identified in 1855 as one of a series of Indian tribes.

CHERRY STREET: This street was named for the fruit in 1857; an adjacent street is Plum.

CHESTER STREET: Originally Perch Street, the name was changed in 1883. It could refer to Chester Arthur, United States President at this time, or to Chester Hitchcock who platted an addition to West St. Paul in 1859, or both.

CHESTNUT STREET: Following a pattern of tree names established in Philadelphia, this, like the adjacent streets, was named in 1849.
    At one time, in the 1850's, there was a creek flowing along the course of Chestnut Street. Called Rice's Brook, it drained at least two lakes: Larpenteur's Lake was between Dale, St. Albans, Carroll and Marshall avenues; the second unnamed lake was between Central, Aurora, St. Albans and Grotto streets. The creek took its name from the Rice brothers, Henry and Edmund, who owned property in the area.

CHILCOMBE AVENUE: The village in Dorset County, England, provided this name in 1885.

CHILDS ROAD: Born in Fergus Falls, James A. Childs (1886-1935) graduated from the University of Minnesota as a civil engineer in 1909. He subsequently worked as a sanitary engineer with the State Board of Health until 1927 when he became chief engineer of the Metropolitan Drainage Commission, forerunner of today's Metropolitan Waste Control Commission. A sixteen-million dollar sewage disposal plant, planned by Childs, was under construction when this street was named by the City Council in 1937.

CHIPPEWA AVENUE: One of a series of Indian names, this street refers to the Chippewa or Ojibway tribe who, at one

time, extended from northern New York to Minnesota. The
Chippewa and the Sioux were the two Indian tribes living
in Minnesota.

CHRISTIE PLACE: Previously part of Prosperity Avenue,
the name was changed in 1940. Who Christie may be is not
recalled or recorded.

CHURCHILL STREET: Part of Warrendale, a development by
Cary Warren of Louisville, Kentucky, this street was named
in 1885.

CLARENCE STREET: Platted in 1886, this street name is said
to remember Clarence Bergman (1882-1933) whose father,
Solomon, came to St. Paul in 1867 where he had a hide and
tallow company.

CLARK STREET: This street was named in 1855 for Martin D.
Clark, a carpenter, who built over two-hundred houses in
the early days of St. Paul. Born in Ohio in 1824, Clark
moved to St. Paul in 1851.

CLAY STREET: Previously Olive and Prince Street, the name
was changed in 1872, perhaps in honor of Henry Clay,
American statesman.

CLAYLAND PLACE AND CLAYLAND STREET: First platted as
Eleanor Street (for the wife of Samuel Tatum) in 1885, the
name was changed the following year to avoid duplication.
The new name corresponded with that of Clayland Park, named
in the original plat.

CLEAR AVENUE: Added to the city in 1889, the meaning of
this unusual name remains unclear.

CLERMONT STREET: Platted as Ravine Street, the name was
changed in 1872. Clermont was the name of the steamboat
designed and used by Robert Fulton on his first trip (1807)
from New York to Albany, thus beginning steam navigation.
To a river city like St. Paul, this was a significant name.

CLEVELAND AVENUE: Grover Cleveland was President of the
United States when this street was named in 1886 as part of
Merriam Park. Cleveland Avenue marks, on the land survey,
a section line.

CLIFF STREET: Originally called Bluff Street, the name was
changed in 1883 to eliminate duplication. The new name was
chosen, obviously, for the steep cliff on the south side of
the street.

CLIFFORD STREET: Like the other streets in the vicinity,
this one was named in 1887 for a village in Massachusetts.

CLIFTON STREET: Originally John Street, the name was changed in 1872, probably for the presence of a cliff at the north end of the street.

CLINTON AVENUE: This was a popular name of the nineteenth century, and it may have been chosen here, in 1855, for its sound.

CLOUGH STREET: David Marston Clough (1846-1924) was Governor of Minnesota from 1895-1899, but it was for his participation in the management of the Minnesota State Agricultural Society that this street within the Fairgrounds is named for him. A Minneapolis resident active in the lumbering business, Clough served as President of the Society in 1891. It was his observation that "It is not necessary to have six days of good weather to make the Fair a financial success. Four days, with a good management, will always pay our bills."

CLOVERLEAF LANE: This name was bestowed by the St. Paul City Council in 1961.

COHANSEY STREET: This street was platted in 1908 by Edward Morton Ware (1834-1918), for many years a real estate and insurance broker in St. Paul, along with his son, Howard F. Ware. Cohansey is the name of a creek and settlement in Cumberland County, New Jersey, where the Ware family settled as early as 1688. The family's handmade chairs were popular with collectors of old American furniture. The New Jersey place name is taken from an early Indian chief.

COLBORNE STREET: At one time Ontario Street and Canada Street, the names were changed in 1872, in reference to the banking village of Colborne, Ontario.

COLBY STREET: The streets in this area (Hiawatha Park) were originally named in 1890 for colleges: Colgate, Cornell, Yale, Colby and Bowdoin. Colby College in Waterville, Maine, was founded in 1813, and is still operating.

COLETTE PLACE: Colette Bisanz was a sister to Leonard and Norbert Bisanz who developed this area in 1951.

COLLEGE AVENUE: This avenue was named in 1851 because it ran by the Episcopal mission and school which had been established the previous year. Their building, the beginning of the Episcopal Church in Minnesota, stood just northeast of Miller Hospital.

COLLINS STREET: Loren C. Collins owned property in the area when this street was named in 1853. He is listed in the 1860 census as a merchant with $10,000 in real estate;

the city directories list him as a dairyman. He was born
about 1813 in Massachusetts; after the Civil War he moved
to Chicago.

COLNE STREET: Colne was a city in Lancaster County,
England, when this street was named in 1885.

COLORADO STREET: Originally John Street, the name was
changed in 1883 to honor the state.

COLUMBUS AVENUE: Added to the city as part of the new
Capitol Approach in 1953, the name was suggested and en-
dorsed by the Knights of Columbus and the Columbus Memorial
Association. There is also a statue of Columbus nearby,
installed in 1931 by the Columbus Memorial Association.

COLVIN AVENUE: Alexander and Sarah Colvin had lived for
many years in the area when this street was named in 1948.
Their house, built about 1909, still stands at 1173 Davern
Avenue behind the Davern house. Standing high on the hill,
it was a landmark for early automobile trips to the area.
Dr. Colvin (1867-1948) was born in Ontario and graduated
from McGill University in Montreal. He immigrated to
St. Paul in 1897; by 1919 he had become chief of instruction
and subsequently, chief of surgery at Ancker Hospital.
Dr. Colvin is said to have owned and operated the first
X-ray machine in St. Paul.

COMMERCIAL STREET: This street was named in 1857 for the
obvious meaning relating to commerce. Adjacent streets
were called Canal and Water.

COMMONWEALTH AVENUE: At one time Dooley Avenue (for Major
James H. Dooley of Richmond, Virginia, one of a group of
capitalists who platted the area), the name was changed in
1902. The present name was first suggested in the annual
report of the Board of Park Commissioners (1901) to apply
to a planned line of parkways stretching from the State
Capitol through Como Park, the Fairgrounds, the Agricultural
College, and branching to the University of Minnesota on one
side, and the Mississippi River Boulevards on the other
side. Since this grand scheme connected both St. Paul and
Minneapolis as well as the state institutions, it was felt
any name should symbolize this relationship; hence the
selection of Commonwealth. The avenue was to be one link
in "this great trunk line of parkways."

COMO AVENUE: Lake Como in northern Italy, near the Swiss
border, is surrounded by mountains and its shores are
bordered by villas. A popular nineteenth century tourist
attraction, its name was borrowed by Henry McKenty to
enhance his real estate around the shores of what had been
known as Sandy Lake. As indicated by its diagonal course,
this avenue, officially named in 1871, follows the route
of an early township road between St. Paul and Como Lake.

The Aldrich Hotel on Lake Como. Built in the 1860's, it burned in 1883. On the farm of William B. Aldrich, the hotel stood on what is today Como Boulevard just north of Horton Avenue.

CONCORD STREET: At one time Cedar Street and Virginia Street, the names were changed in 1876. Concord is the name of historic towns in both Massachusetts and New Hampshire.

CONCORDIA AVENUE: Originally part of Roblyn, Rondo, and Carroll avenues, this street was reconstructed as the southern frontage road to Interstate Highway 94, and re-named in 1964. The new name is derived from Concordia College which has its grounds along this street near Hamline Avenue. The college campus was originally the site of the Minnesota State Reform School founded on a tract called "The Burt Farm" in 1868. Established for the welfare of delinquent minors, the reformatory had at one time over a hundred children in its care. One of the old reform school buildings remained, fronting on Concordia Avenue, until foolishly razed by the college in 1975.

CONGRESS STREET: This street was first named Grove, later Susan, and finally Congress in 1886. Congress is an old street name, from Boston, and eminently suitable in its meaning of joining people together.

CONWAY STREET: Previously named First Street and Levee Street, the name was changed in 1872, in honor of Charles R. Conway. Born in 1822 in Indiana, he drifted to Minnesota in 1849 by way of Michigan, Illinois, and Wisconsin. He was a journalist by profession and managed the Los Angeles News during the Civil War, thus becoming one of the first Minnesotans to leave for California. Of course, he came back to St. Paul. Conway owned much valuable real estate in early St. Paul which brought him no profit, because, according to a contemporary, "He knows how to make money, but he can't get it, because he won't lie and steal."

COOK AVENUE: John B. Cook (1818-1910) was president of the St. Paul Omnibus Company when this street was named in 1872.

COOPER STREET: Born in Pennsylvania, John Francis Cooper (1836-1907) migrated to St. Cloud, Minnesota in 1856 where, over the years, he developed an extensive livestock breeding operation which included a famous herd of Cruikshanks Short Horn cattle. Known as "a very useful member," Cooper was elected to the Board of Managers for the Minnesota State Agricultural Society, the organization responsible for the State Fair and the naming of this street within the Fairgrounds. After his service as a Manager from 1884 to 1891, Cooper was elected President of the Society from 1898 to 1901.

COPLEY AVENUE: Originally platted as Cherry Street, the name was changed later. Why, or by whom, I cannot say.

CORNING AVENUE: Charles T. and Frances Corning platted this street in 1887. He was a brother of John W. L. Corning, with whom he was for a short time a partner in the building materials firm which operates today as Corning-Donohue. Charles came to St. Paul in the 1880's·but died in 1888 at age forty-five. His obituary records the cause of death as pneumonia aggravated by a constitutional weakness produced by overexertion at athletics·.

CORTLAND PLACE: At first New Canada Road, the name was changed to Cortland in 1874. Most of the street running parallel to Oakland Cemetery has since been renamed as Jackson.

COSGROVE STREET: "Whenever a Minnesota farmer sees a
Hereford, he thinks of Cosgrove." Upon that observation,
Carson N. Cosgrove (1853-1936) was elected President of
the Minnesota State Agricultural Society, the organization
responsible for the yearly State Fair, and the naming of
this street within the Fairgrounds. Born in Westfield,
New York, Cosgrove settled in LeSueur, Minnesota, at the
age of eighteen. Well known as a breeder and exhibitor of
Hereford cattle as well as a merchant in hardware and
agricultural machinery, he served as President of the
Society from 1902 to 1907 and as Secretary from 1907 to
1910.

COTTAGE AVENUE: This street name first appears in 1855 in
a development wishfully entitled Homes for the Homeless.

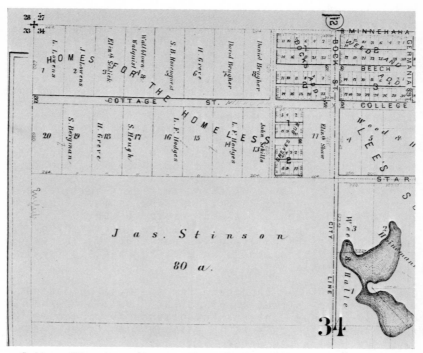

*Cottage Street as it runs through the addition entitled
"Homes for the Homeless."*

COTTONWOOD AVENUE: Platted in 1881, this street was named
for the tree. An adjacent street was called Cedar.

CRAIG PLACE: Craig is the second son of Alexander G.
Tankenoff, president of the Hillcrest Development Company
which platted this area in 1948.

CRETIN AVENUE: Running between the St. Paul Seminary and
St. Thomas College, this street was named in 1890 for
Joseph Cretin (1799-1857), first Bishop of St. Paul. Born,
educated, and ordained in France, Cretin journeyed to
America in 1838 with Bishop Loras of Dubuque, Iowa. The
accounts of his early travels and his description of the
first Cathedral give a vivid impression of early St. Paul.

CROCUS PLACE: Originally part of Dale Street and West
Crocus Hill, the name was changed in 1889. The term comes
from the plat Crocus Hill which is said to have been given
by James Taylor to the hill because of the many crocus
flowers that bloomed there in the early spring.

CROMWELL AVENUE: Oliver Cromwell (1599-1658), chief
leader of England for some years, is honored by this street
named in 1885 as part of St. Anthony Park.

CULLEN STREET: In 1872, the Protestant Orphan Asylum of
St. Paul purchased, for $29,000, the Cullen farm comprising
thirty-six acres of land, a large stone house, and stone
barn. Failing to raise the money to pay off the three-year
mortgage, part of the farm was platted into building lots
in 1874 when this street was named. By 1885 the house was
too small, and the Asylum moved into a new building on the
southeast corner of Marshall and St. Albans streets.
     The Cullen farm was the property of Major William J.
Cullen (1817-1870) who came to St. Paul in 1857 as Superintendent of Indian Affairs. His house, an elaborate
French style mansion built in 1861, remains, greatly remodeled, at 698 Stewart Avenue. Cullen was remembered as
a "man of great force of character, self-reliant, original,
positive, persuasive, ambitious, and he moved about more
like a young elephant than an ordinary man."
     Cullen Street, which had several houses along its
length before the railroad was constructed, is now only a
dirt track cutting across an area known historically as
the Bay Triangle.

CULVERT STREET: A candidate for the most unimaginative
name given any street in all of St. Paul, this one was
named in 1886 by John and Susan Wagener. The name had
reference to the culvert in which Phalen Creek flowed out
of Swede Hollow and under East Seventh Street. Residents
of Swede Hollow, in cleaning up the creek, considered the
task completed when the debris had been pushed down the
Hollow and into this culvert, where it was out of sight
and would eventually be washed away.

CUMBERLAND STREET: Like Cohansey, this street was platted
in 1908 by Edwin M. Ware. Cumberland is a county in New
Jersey, containing the settlement of Cohansey, where the
Ware family lived.

CURFEW STREET: Added in 1888, the name indicates the retirement of people from the streets into their homes; perhaps there is a little metaphor implicit in the word.

CURTICE STREET: Born in New York, David L. Curtice (1828-1902) traveled to St. Paul in 1856 where he worked with James A. Case, city engineer when this street was named in 1858. A surveyor, engineer, and map maker, Curtice was later appointed city engineer from 1869 to 1874, and it was upon his recommendation that Baptist Hill, a fifty-foot embankment in the vicinity of Mears Park, was leveled.

CURVE STREET: This street was named in 1913 because of its diagonal course along the St. Paul and White Bear Electric Railway. There was a train station on the northeast corner of Maryland and Hazel streets.

"SWEDE HOLLOW"

"Swedes, Irish, Italians, Pole, Mexicans--each nationality helped amplify the congestion and unsanitary conditions to a point which finally brought drastic action."

CUSTER STREET: Originally Clay Street, the name was changed
in 1876. The name honors General George A. Custer, U.S. Army
officer, who, along with his 264 men, was killed in the
battle of Little Bighorn on June 25, 1876. Needless to say,
popular sentiment was on Custer's side, and he became a
national hero by the time this street was named four months
later.

CUTLER STREET: William Jonathan Cutler of Boston had,
shortly after the Civil War, a one-hundred acre farm in
this location. Named "Fairoaks," the farm served as an
investment and summer health resort for the family.
William's son, Edward, stayed in St. Paul to become a
partner in the wholesale firm of Noyes Brothers and Cutler.
This street was named in 1959 by the City Council.

CYPRESS STREET: One of the many tree names, this street,
originally platted as Boston Street, was renamed in 1872.

D

DALE STREET: This name suddenly appears, in 1871, on a number of maps. It was at that time St. Paul's western boundary. Because the land in the area was far more irregular then, the name probably indicated a valley or depression.

DALY STREET: Thomas Daly, the developer of this street in 1857, was a well-to-do young man from Canada. He did not remain in St. Paul long, and little can be learned of him.

DANFORTH STREET: Willis and Nancy Ann Danforth of Milwaukee, Wisconsin, platted this street in 1885.

DANIEL STREET: Originally Water Street, the name was changed in 1876. The significance of this new name, if any, is not apparent.

DARLENE STREET: This street was opened by the city in 1954, but the identity of Darlene is a mystery.

DAVERN STREET: William Davern (1831-1913) immigrated from Ireland to America in 1848, and to St. Paul the following year. He purchased a 160 acre farm between today's Snelling, Fairview, Montreal and St. Paul avenues, where he built his house about the time of the Civil War. This house still stands, although greatly remodeled, at 1173 Davern Street. A farmer and dairyman, Davern at one time owned all of Pike Island. The original "Davern Road" ran from his house down to West Seventh Street; it was extended north and became a city street in 1887.

DAVID STREET: Opened by the city in 1954, this street was named for the grandson of Herbert S. West, a plat commissioner at the time.

DAVIS STREET: Previously Benton Street, the name was changed to avoid duplication in 1886. Davis is a common personal and place name - short, easy to pronounce and spell. There may have been a passing thought for Cushman K. Davis, Governor of Minnesota from 1874-1876.

Hon. LYMAN DAYTON,

"Sonny"

DAYTON AVENUE: This street was named in 1854 for Lyman
Dayton (1810-1865), one of the leading real estate specu-
lators of early St. Paul. Dayton's Bluff is named for him,
as is the town of Dayton in Hennepin County. Maria and
Bates avenues are named for his wife. Born in Connecticut,
Dayton worked as a merchant in Providence, Rhode Island,
before coming to St. Paul in 1849.
        In a revealing sketch, written some fifty years after
his death, Dayton is described as six feet tall and weighing
300 pounds, attired in an outfit consisting of a high hat
with immense brim, a long coat, a velvet vest with white
embroidery, and a colossal watch chain. He was popularly
known as "Sonny," a nickname he detested; he once set a man
upon a red hot stove for calling him that. Dayton was at
one time arrested for assault with a pistol, and also quar-
reled frequently with his mother, sometimes beating her
until she would deed her property over to him. Often in
financial difficulty, Dayton usually kept his land in the
name of a third party so it could not be confiscated by
his creditors.

Notwithstanding these eccentricities, another source recalls him as a man "possessed of great energy, kind-hearted, and public spirited." In either case, he was an important figure in the development of St. Paul, and had he lived into the real estate boom of the 1870's, he would have been one of its richest men. The present day department store family is not directly related.

Bank notes, printed by Lyman Dayton, in 1850. Issued because of a lack of currency in frontier St. Paul, they were based largely on Dayton's real estate holdings, and were generally known as "wildcat money."

DEALTON STREET: Ivan and Catherine Kipp applied this street name in 1912. It is said to be that of De Alton or Alton D. Smith, one of a family that farmed in the area.

DE COURCY DRIVE: Elizabeth De Courcy was a St. Paul Councilwoman from 1956-1962, and Ramsey County Commissioner from 1967-1974. This street was named in 1956.

DELANO PLACE: Platted as Calvin Street, the name was changed to avoid conflict with Colvin Street nearby. Renamed in 1950, the name may be a passing reference to Franklin Delano Roosevelt.

DELAWARE AVENUE: This is one of a series of Indian names applied in 1855.

DELLRIDGE AVENUE: See Berland Place.

DELOS STREET: Delos A. Monfort (1835-1899), a prominent banker of the city, first traveled through St. Paul in 1854 and returned here in 1857. Beginning with Mackubin and Edgerton in their banking house, he subsequently became cashier for the Second National Bank with which he remained off and on for the remainder of his life.

    In the early part of his career as a banker, Monfort,
in order to stop a run on his bank, made an extraordinary
trip to St. Peter. As St. Paul Historian Henry Castle
relates:

> *It was known that the Nicollet County Bank*
> *had at St. Peter about $5,000 in gold, as*
> *a redemption fund. Every bank dispatched*
> *a swift messenger to St. Peter with all of*
> *the notes on the Nicollet County institution*
> *that could be readily obtained. The People's*
> *Bank secured the prize. Its messenger,*
> *D. A. Monfort, gathered up about $5,000 of*
> *the Nicollet bank notes and set out for*
> *St. Peter on horseback. Riding three horses*
> *to exhaustion and not drawing bridle save to*
> *make the relays, he passed every other carrier*
> *on the road and made the seventy-eight miles*
> *in eight hours. He secured the gold. He was*
> *greatly fatigued, but the following morning*
> *he set out and returned to St. Paul just in*
> *time. There was a "run" on the People's Bank,*
> *and the last dollar was in sight when cashier*
> *Monfort staggered in with his heavy pair of*
> *saddle bags. The reinforcement was believed*
> *to consist of $25,000 instead of $5,000. The*
> *"run" subsided and was soon over.*

    Tradition has it that Delos ate standing up at the
fireplace mantel the following week.

DENSLOW STREET: This street was named in 1892, probably for
LeGrand N. Denslow, the developer, and a professor at the
St. Paul Medical College. His brother was W. W. Denslow,
well-known illustrator of the Wizard of Oz.

DESNOYER AVENUE: Although the area was platted in 1887 as
Desnoyer Park, there was no street by this name until 1919
when Maplewood Avenue was changed to Desnoyer Avenue.
Stephen Desnoyer (1805-1877) was born in St. Johns, Canada.
He was subsequently a farmer in New York State, a clothier
in St. Louis, and a lumber merchant in Dubuque, before
coming to St. Paul in 1843. He took a claim of 320 acres
between Cleveland Avenue, the river, Marshall, and St.
Anthony avenues, and thus became the first white settler
in the Midway area.

DeSOTO STREET: This street was named in 1853 for the
Spanish explorer, Hernando de Soto, who discovered the
Mississippi River.

DEUBENER PLACE: Originally Roebe Street, the name was
changed in 1940 to avoid conflict with Robie Street.
Walter H. Deubener is a long-time resident of the city

who, about 1916, invented the shopping bag in his grocery store on Seventh Street. He subsequently established a factory in Indianapolis to manufacture them. Deubener owned extensive real estate within the city, including an apartment building on this street.

DEWEY STREET: At one time Laura Avenue, the name was changed in 1898 to avoid conflict with Laurel Avenue. Admiral George Dewey (1837-1917) destroyed the entire Spanish fleet during the Spanish-American War, a feat which made him a national hero overnight.

DIETER STREET: William F. Dieter (1828-1896) ran a shoe store in St. Paul for many years. Born in Germany, he immigrated to St. Paul in 1854 and was active in business circles here for the remainder of his life. This street was named in 1887.

DOANE AVENUE: Some of the streets in this area were named in 1887 for towns in Massachusetts, or surrounding states. Doane may be one of these towns, or it may be a personal name selected because of its pleasing sound. I do not think it has any local significance.

DODD ROAD: William B. Dodd (1811-1862) was born in New Jersey where he was educated as a machinist and later became a civil engineer. Moving to Minnesota in 1850 as a member of a land company, he platted the city of St. Peter in 1854, and built the first house there. With the future of his city in mind, he laid out a sixty-five mile road from St. Peter to St. Paul which was later adopted for use by the government. Dodd was killed in defending New Ulm against the Sioux attack in 1862.

DONOHUE AVENUE: Originally Bohn Street, the name was changed in 1957 to honor John H. Donohue II (1883-1956). Mr. Donohue was a founder, in 1916, of the building materials firm, Corning-Donohue, Incorporated. The firm was located on this street from 1955 to 1970.

DORA LANE: Herbert and Dorothy Halverson platted this street in 1949.

DOROTHEA AVENUE: Dorothea was the wife of Norbert Bisanz, one of the Bisanz brothers who developed this area in 1951.

DOSWELL AVENUE: Brooke Doswell of Fredericksburg, Virginia, helped finance this plat in 1885.

DOUGLAS STREET: Stephen A. Douglas (1813-1861) was United States Senator from Illinois who, as chairman of the Committee on Territories, advocated the formation of the Minnesota Territory in 1848. The street was named the following year. Douglas is perhaps best known as the candidate whom Abraham Lincoln defeated for President in 1860.

DOUGLYNN LANE: This street was named in 1959 for the two
children of Jene and Gloria Sigvertsen who had purchased a
building lot at the end of the street.   Before building on
the property, however, Sigvertsen, an architect, sold the
lot to live elsewhere in the area.

DOUSMAN STREET: Hercules L. Dousman (1800-1868) of
Prairie du Chien, Wisconsin, an agent of the American Fur
Company, had extensive property holdings throughout the
state.   He is credited as being the first to suggest the
name Minnesota for the new territory.   This street name
was assigned in 1851.

DRAKE STREET: Elias F. Drake (1813-1892) was born in Ohio
and practiced law and banking there until 1852 when he
began building railroads.   In 1862, he brought the first
train to Minnesota.   He was later President of the St. Paul
and Sioux City Railroad whose track and shops were adjacent
to this street named in 1880.

DREWRY LANE: Previously part of Payne Avenue, the street
was renamed in 1933 when Payne was rerouted.   Edward
Drewry (1829-1926) was born in Reading, England; he
journeyed to St. Paul in 1857 where he opened an ale and
porter bottling house at Dayton's Bluff.   Ten years later
he moved his business to a location on present-day Drewry
Lane.   The company flourished over the years, until
Prohibition when the firm turned to producing soft drinks.
Edward's son sold the family business in 1932, although it
continued under the Drewry name until 1952.   A second son
went to Winnipeg in 1875, and founded a branch of the
company there which grew to be the largest brewery in
western Canada.

DUCHESS STREET: At one time Greenwood Street, the name was
changed in 1887.   Duchess, with an agreeable sound, and a
suggestion of royalty, is short and easy to pronounce.

DUDLEY AVENUE: This is a common place and family name in
England.   English names, though without local significance,
were popular in the 1880's.

DUKE STREET: Thomas Daly, a well-to-do young man from
Canada, named three streets in 1856:   Duke, Richmond, and
Canada.   The obvious inference would be that they honored
the Fourth Duke of Richmond, one-time Governor General of
Canada, who died from the bite of a pet fox.

DULUTH STREET: Originally Phalen Street, the name was
changed in 1885.   The northern boundary of this street was
the St. Paul and Duluth Railroad.

DUNEDIN TERRACE: Previously Isabel Street, the name was
changed around 1900.

<u>DUNLAP STREET</u>:   William Dunlap (1833-1901) was a builder and real estate dealer here after 1885.   One of Dunlap's residences, a fine Civil War era house, still stands at 531 Brainerd Avenue.

E

EAGLE STREET: Serving "upper town," which was the area between Wabasha Street and Seven Corners, one of the city's two major steamboat landings was at the foot of Eagle Street. The eagle was a popular symbol of the United States when this street was named in 1849, and its image graces many buildings and towns.

EARL STREET: Platted as East Street in 1857, the name was changed in 1872. It is a personal name; whose I cannot say.

EAST STREET: This street ran on the east side of the plat when it was opened in 1892.

EAST SHORE DRIVE: Originally Overbrook Avenue, the name was changed in 1926 when the Drive was extended further along the east shore of Lake Phalen.

EATON STREET: "A sort of general locomotive crushing down all obstacles in his way," Samuel S. Eaton (1825-1899) was born in Vermont and traveled to California in 1849 by way of Canada. From there, he moved to Buffalo, New York and came to St. Paul in 1855 where he engaged in the insurance business for the remainder of his life. It is said he wrote the first insurance policy in Minnesota, and was the first secretary of the St. Paul Fire and Marine Insurance Company. The developer of this property in 1857, Eaton is remembered as being "earnest in what he does." His house, built 116 years ago, still stands at 468 Hopkins Street.

EBERTZ COURT: Walter J. Ebertz of St. Paul named this
street in 1972 for his father, William Ebertz (1884-1952)
who was also a contractor.

ECHO AVENUE: Echo was the wife of Edwin Johnson who was
associated with the real estate firm making this plat in
1946.

EDGAR AVENUE: Several parties from Stillwater named this
street in 1904. Who Edgar was, I cannot say.

EDGCUMBE ROAD: This city parkway was first platted as Summit
Avenue South, and projected as an extension to Summit Avenue.
The present name was given in 1912 by Charles B. Dunn,
Philadelphia banker and owner of the property, for his home
in Chestnut Hill, Pennsylvania which, in turn, was named for
Mount Edgcumbe in his native Cornwall, England. In the over-
all scheme of city parkways, Edgcumbe Road is a link between
Lexington Parkway on the east, and the Mississippi River
Boulevard on the west.

EDGEBROOK AVENUE: Platted as Eastview Avenue in 1960, the
name was changed two years later. Both names were picked
to fit the alphabetical sequence of the area.

EDGEMONT STREET: This fancy name applied in 1887 gives the
impression of height, view, mountains, etc.

EDGERTON STREET: Born in New York state where he worked for
a time as a fearless deputy sheriff, Erastus S. Edgerton
(1816-1893) moved to St. Paul in 1853. He opened a bank here
with money inherited from his father's estate and spent the
remainder of his life in banking interests. Upon his retirement, he returned to New York City where he was often seen
riding his Kentucky bred horse in Central Park. This street,
originally called Miller Street, was renamed for Edgerton in
1872.

EDGEWATER BOULEVARD: A popular name when it was added to the
city in 1946, this street follows the west edge of Beaver
Lake.

EDMUND AVENUE: Remembered as a kind and generous man of
placid disposition, Edmund Rice (1819-1889) must be considered one of St. Paul's finest citizens. Born in Vermont,
he came to Minnesota in 1849 after serving various legal
capacities in Michigan. A member of the legislature for
several terms, he was also a County Commissioner and twice
Mayor of St. Paul. His activities in various railroad
companies earned him the nickname "father of Minnesota
railroading." As a leading land speculator and developer,
he named several streets for members of his family. In
spite of his many achievements, however, Rice's later years
were spent close to poverty.

EDMUND RICE
"a most generous nature and a kind heart"

EICHENWALD STREET: John M. Keller (1833-1896) platted this
street in 1877 and named it for his large estate and house
on what is today the north corner of Sixth and Eichenwald
streets. That name comes from Keller's German birthplace,
a small village near Dresden. Keller, a master carpenter,
ran a lumber yard for many years, and his son, Herbert P.
Keller, was Mayor of St. Paul from 1910-1914.

"EICHENWALD"
RESIDENCE of JOHN M. KELLER, DAYTON'S BLUFF, ST. PAUL, MINN.

EIGHTH STREET: One of the earliest St. Paul street names
dating from 1849, this eighth street from the river was
the location of many of the city brothels in the 1880's.

ELEANOR AVENUE: Horace and Mary Rugg named this street in
1882. Their house remains at 251 Summit Avenue, but the
identity of Eleanor has been lost.

ELEVENTH STREET: Named in 1850, this was the eleventh street
from the river.

ELFELT STREET: Abram S. Elfelt (1827-1888) and Charles D.
Elfelt (1828-1899) opened the first dry goods store in
St. Paul in 1849. Their second store, built in 1851, stood
at the corner of Third and Exchange streets and was at the
time the largest building in the city. The upper floor of
this building became St. Paul's first theatre. The street
was named in 1855.

ELIZABETH STREET: What woman, if any, prompted this name in 1855 I cannot say.

ELK STREET: This street was named in 1870 for the animal; an adjacent street is Buffalo.

ELLIOT PLACE: Other than a nice English sound, this name, applied in 1933, does not seem to have any particular significance.

ELLIS AVENUE: Without doubt, this is a personal name, perhaps that of an investor in St. Anthony Park when this street was named in 1885.

ELM STREET: Eighty percent of the towns in the Midwest have at least one street named for a tree. It is interesting to speculate that today, few city dwellers could distinguish one species of tree from another.

ELMWOOD STREET: Named in 1888.

ELSIE LANE: Elsie was the wife of Den E. Lane, probably St. Paul's leading land developer in the 1920's and 1930's. He platted large areas of Highland Park and the area around Lake Phalen, including this street which he named in 1950. One has to admire him for not taking advantage of his name to proliferate Lanes throughout the city.

ELWAY STREET: It is most likely that some individual prompted this street name in 1881.

EMERALD STREET: With its associations of green, suggesting growth and plants, the emerald stone was the impetus for this 1886 street name.

EMMA STREET: There were a number of developers in this 1879 addition; none of them was named Emma.

EMPSON ALLEY: An obscure byway, this alley and its name honor the author of this series -- a kind, scholarly individual who wishes no more than to quietly pass through life patiently researching Orphic conundrums and perplexing enigmas.

ENDICOTT STREET: This street, named in 1885 as part of St. Anthony Park, commemorates John Endicott (1589?-1665), several times governor and official of the Massachusetts Bay Colony, one of the first settlements in this country.

ENGLEWOOD AVENUE: Previously Capitol Avenue, the name was changed in 1940. The significance of this new name, if any, is neither recalled nor recorded.

ENGLISH STREET: In 1880 when this street was named, William H. English (1822-1896) was the Democratic candidate

for the Vice-Presidency as the running mate of General
Winfield Hancock. Streets were named for both candidates
by the developer, Franz Sigel, a Civil War general who
lived in New York City at this time.
   English Street from Arlington north to County Road B
follows the course of the Lake Phalen-White Bear Road which
was laid out during the Civil War. This road came northeast
from downtown St. Paul, around the south end of Lake Phalen,
and north on English Street.

ERIE STREET: Originally First Street, the name was changed
in 1872. It is, like Superior and Michigan streets which
it intersects, named for one of the Great Lakes.

ESCANABA AVENUE: Escanaba is a Chippewa word meaning "land
of the red buck." In this instance however, it was probably
borrowed, in 1917, directly from the river and city in
Michigan of the same name, without regard for its literal
meaning.

ESTABROOK DRIVE: John D. Estabrook, a civil engineer by
profession, was the first Superintendent of Parks in St.
Paul, a position he held less than a year between 1888-1889.
The City Council honored him in 1967 by this street name
within Como Park.

ETHEL STREET: Previously named Commercial Street, the name
was changed in 1876.

OSSIAN EUCLID DODGE
"The eccentric troubadour"

ETNA STREET: Platted as John Street, the name was changed
to avoid duplication in 1872. Etna is a volcano in Sicily
and the name may have been chosen because of the street's
position on the hill.

EUCLID STREET: Labeled by one historian as the "eccentric
troubadour," Ossian Euclid Dodge (1820-1876) was a nationally
known vocalist, journalist, and composer of popular music.
When his music store on Euclid Street in Cleveland, Ohio,
failed, and his literary interests brought him little profit,
he moved to St. Paul in 1862. Here he built a house which
he called Alpine Cottage, sold pianos, and speculated in
real estate, naming this street in 1873. Dodge also acted
as the correspondent for a local newspaper in reporting the
gold rush of northern Minnesota, and served as secretary of
the St. Paul Chamber of Commerce. However, Dodge's personality made him enemies, and a scandalous divorce gave him
reason to sail for England where he died two years later.

EUSTIS STREET: Samuel S. Eustis (1815-1884) and his wife,
Emily Clark Eustis (1819-1909) had a farm directly west of
this street named in 1885 as part of St. Anthony Park.
Samuel was born in Maine, Emily in New Hampshire; together
they came to Minnesota with their children in 1855,
settling at "Groveland" as the Midway area was then called.
In 1867, they bought 200 acres (at fourteen dollars an acre)
in an area today roughly west of Highway 280, and north of
University Avenue. Their farmhouse, built in 1872, still
stands at 3107 Fourth Street, S.E., but it is now converted
to apartments. The farm land was gradually sold off in the
1880's and 1890's for railroad and commercial use at prices
of $1000-$2000 an acre.

EVA STREET: Originally named Goodhue Street, the name was
changed in 1876 to avoid duplication. Feminine names were
popular on the West Side.

EVERETT COURT: This is probably a personal name, perhaps
that of an investor in St. Anthony Park when this street
was named in 1885.

EVERGREEN PLACE: Intended as part of a connection between
Summit Avenue and Edgcumbe Road, this street was given a
separate name in 1917, because it was then, and still is,
entirely within the confines of Park Nursery. Although
never graded, it remains a public street.

EXCHANGE STREET: This street was named in 1849, probably
for the commercial implications of the name, as in stock
exchange, grain exchange, and the like.

EXETER PLACE: Previously part of Marlboro Avenue, the name
was changed as part of a general renaming within this area
in 1922. Exeter is a common English name without much
significance in this case.

FAIR PLACE: The street's proximity to the State Fairgrounds prompted this name in 1913.

FAIRMOUNT AVENUE: Part of the Highland Park Addition, this street was named in 1883 for the pleasing sound and its location on Crocus Hill. Fair is a common prefix; mount gives the suggestion of height.

FAIRVIEW AVENUE: There have been several streets within the city bearing this nondescript name at one time or another. The present one was named in 1886 as part of Howard Park.

FALCON AVENUE: See Berland Place.

FARRINGTON STREET: Considered reticent and undemonstrative, but an excellent businessman, John Farrington (1827-1905) was born in Ireland. He journeyed to the United States about 1833 and to St. Paul in 1850. After constructing the first brick store in the city, he engaged in the fur trade business, and subsequently sold real estate, naming this street in 1854. He was also a member of the Board of Public Works for several years.

FAUQUIER PLACE: Applied as a street name here in 1857,
Fauquier is a county in Virginia, the home of Rice W. Payne,
for whom Payne Avenue is named.

FAYE STREET: Faye (Mrs. Ernest H.) Williams worked for a
local nursing home; her husband worked for the police department. Both were friends of Grege Beckett, Plat Commissioner when this street was named in 1965. Kim Place
is named for the Williams' daughter.

FELLOWS LANE: The Housing and Redevelopment Authority named
this street in 1951 for Lieutenant Reid F. Fellows of the
Army Air Corps who was killed in Italy in 1943. This entire
housing project was dedicated to those who died in the
Second World War.

FERDINAND STREET: Originally named Willius Street, the name
was changed in 1886 to avoid duplication. Ferdinand Willius
(1830-1916) was a banker and one-time member of the City
Council. (See Willius Street.)

FERNWOOD STREET: This very common name was applied in 1916.
Fern implies coolness, and wood is a popular suffix.

FERONIA AVENUE: This street name, like the others in Union
Park, was almost surely chosen in 1884 for its pleasing and
somewhat exotic sound. Feronia contains the sound of fern,
with its connotations of a shaded, quiet place.

FIELD AVENUE: Emil A. Field was the President, and
J. H. Field, Secretary, of the Northwestern Lumber and
Wrecking Company of Minneapolis who platted this Homecroft
Addition in 1907. Croft is an old English word meaning
enclosure; it was a popular suffix at the time.

FIFIELD STREET: Fifield is a lumbering village in Price
County, Wisconsin, named for Lieutenant Governor S. S.
Fifield of Ashland. Two of the St. Anthony Park investors
were in the Wisconsin lumber business when this street was
named in 1885.

FILLMORE AVENUE: McCarthy Street, the original name, was
changed in 1883. The present name is most likely a reference
to Millard Fillmore (1800-1874), President of the United
States from 1850 to 1853.

FINN STREET: William Finn (1819-1889) was the first permanent white settler in this area. Born in Ireland, he
came to the United States and enlisted in the Mexican War.
In 1848, as a result of his military service, he received
a grant of land extending from today's Marshall Avenue to
St. Clair Avenue, and Fairview Avenue to the river. He
built his house where St. Thomas College now stands, and
farmed the adjacent property. Later he sold his farm to
the Catholic Church for an Industrial School, and it was

Archbishop Ireland who bestowed this street name in 1889 within the Groveland plat.

FIR STREET: Previously Bellevue Street, the name was changed in 1940.

FISK STREET: Born in New York, James L. Fisk (1835-1902) came to Minnesota in the 1850's. He rose to the rank of Captain in the Civil War, and subsequently led expeditions to the gold fields of Montana. This street was named in 1872.

FLANDRAU STREET: Remembered as a "first-class lawyer and a first-class man," Charles E. Flandrau (1828-1903) was a judge, soldier, and author. Born in New York City where he studied law in his father's office, he moved to St. Paul in 1853 as a lawyer. Four years later, he was an influential member of the Minnesota Constitutional Convention, after which he was appointed Associate Justice of the Minnesota Supreme Court. Flandrau was Commander of the defense of New Ulm during the Sioux Uprising, and later an unsuccessful candidate for Governor. Upon his retirement, he wrote several books on the history of Minnesota. This street was named in his honor in 1886.

FLORENCE AVENUE: William and Carrie Johnson of Ramsey County added this street to the city in 1910. Florence is most likely connected with that family, but it would be impossible to locate her among all the Johnsons.

FLORIDA STREET: Previously Eighth Street, the name was changed in 1876. Like the adjacent streets, it was named for a state.

FLYNN STREET: Known as "the confidant of half of the Court House and City Hall," Hilary J. Flynn (1898-1954) was born in St. Paul. Educated at St. Thomas College, and admitted to the Bar in 1922, Flynn subsequently became prosecuting attorney for the city. He was honored by this street name in 1956, however, for his career with the city as research bureau director where he helped develop ordinances, gave the City Council background material, and aided in representing the city to the legislature.

FOLSOM STREET: Considered "tenacious as an old hickory tree" Simeon Pearl Folsom (1819-1907) was city Plat Commissioner when this street was named in 1887. A true pioneer of the city, Folsom was born in Canada, grew up in New Hampshire, and roamed the West before coming to St. Paul in 1847. Here he took up the real estate business and became city surveyor in 1854. He founded the first abstract and title company in the city, served in various civic posts, fought in the Civil War, later worked extensively for the railroads, and served as attorney for the St. Paul water commissioners.

FORBES AVENUE: William Henry Forbes (1815-1875) was a clerk
for the American Fur Company post at Mendota when this street
was named in 1849. He became a resident of St. Paul in 1847
when the city had five stores, about twenty families, and
thirty-six children, composed of French, English, Swiss,
Sioux, Chippewa, and African descent, making the total popu-
lation no more than fifty. Forbes--impulsive, kind-hearted,
generous, social--served in the Civil War and later was the
Indian agent at Devil's Lake, North Dakota.

FORBES & KITTSON,

Corner Third and Roberts Streets,

SAINT PAUL, - MINNESOTA.

WHOLESALE AND RETAIL DEALERS IN

Indian Goods, Furs and Pelts.

ALSO A LARGE ASSORTMENT OF

FANCY DRY GOODS.

THE HIGHEST MARKET PRICE PAID FOR FURS AND PELTS.

Forbes' advertisement as seen in the 1856 St. Paul Business Directory

FORD PARKWAY: Originally platted, in part, as St. Catherine
Avenue, the name was changed to Edsel Avenue and, in 1924,
to Ford Road. Both Edsel and Ford are references to the
Ford Motor Company which purchased 160 acres of land on which
to build their assembly plant. Interestingly enough, the

Cars manufactured at the Ford Plant are loaded onto barges in the Mississippi River below the factory.

purchase of this land was contingent upon obtaining the
water power from Lock and Dam Number 1 (Ford Dam) which
had been built shortly before to aid river navigation into
Minneapolis. The Ford Motor Company leased the electricity
generated by the water falling over the dam, and have used
it to provide electricity for their assembly plant for over
fifty years.

FOREST STREET: Applied in 1857, this street name has an
obvious meaning: a dense growth of trees and underbrush.
Adjacent streets were Birch, Elm, and Hazel.

FOREST HILL AVENUE: The most common element of street names
gives the impression of height; the second most common gives
the impression of forest, trees, and woods. It is as though
everyone would like to live on a wooded hill. This 1888
street name combines both elements to give a pleasant, but
trite, effect.

FORESTER STREET: Previously unnamed, this street was so
designated in 1887. This is a fairly common surname; whether
one individual is signified, I cannot say.

FOSTER STREET: This street was named in 1918 as part of the
Midway Industrial Division. Other streets were named for
local businessmen, but who Foster might be is uncertain.

FOUNTAIN PLACE: Originally part of Preble Street, the name
was changed in 1890. In front of the only home on the street,
Number 614, is an artificial series of waterfalls descending
down Swede Hollow into a large stone pool. The whole is
graced with stone fences, walkways, terraces, and, to one
side, a wrought iron rose trellis. Adjacent to the house,
overhanging Swede Hollow, is a ramshackle building, once an
artist's studio. Built almost a century ago by a previous
owner of the house, the whole arrangement has not been used
for decades.

FOURTEENTH STREET: Platted in 1856, this is the fourteenth
street from the river.

FOURTH STREET: One of the most interesting passageways of
the city is Fourth Street, running east from Broadway,
across and under the railroad tracks to Commercial Street
below Mounds Park. This is the route of the first road
east out of St. Paul to Point Douglas where the St. Croix
and Mississippi rivers meet. Under the railroad tracks,
beneath an old limestone bridge, Trout Brook comes to the
surface, and flows to the river. This brook, an important
geographical feature in the development of St. Paul, begins
at McCarron's Lake and, running through the city, provided
the impetus for several early mills. Today the stream is
largely obliterated, the water running through the storm
sewers, except where it surfaces on Fourth Street. This
street, the fourth from the river, was named in 1849.

FOXRIDGE ROAD: As the developer put it, this 1970 name just sounded nice.

FRANK STREET: William Dawson, Robert Smith and John Terry platted this street in 1873. Frank was a son of John Terry (1824-1902).

FRANKLIN AVENUE: Previously Bayard Street, the name was changed in 1926 as a continuation of the Minneapolis avenue.

FRANKSON AVENUE: Thomas Frankson (1869-1939) was Lieutenant Governor of Minnesota from 1917-1921. Born in Fillmore County, he graduated from the University of Minnesota Law School in 1900. Returning to his home in Spring Valley, Minnesota he entered the real estate business where he had far flung investments. Frankson later served in the state legislature, and purchased property around Como Park which he developed, naming this street in 1913. A resident of St. Paul in his later years, Frankson's house, built about 1915, remains at 1349 Midway Parkway.

FRED STREET: This street was named in 1882 for Fred M. Turnbull, son of George and Amanda Turnbull, the developers.

FREDERICK STREET: Frederick was the son of Thomas B. and Louisa Campbell, the developers of this street in 1887.

FREMONT AVENUE: Originally Hazel Street, the name was changed in 1872 to honor John C. Fremont (1813-1890) "the pathfinder," an American soldier, explorer, and politician. In 1856 and 1864 he was a presidential candidate and later served as Governor of the Arizona Territory.

FRONT AVENUE: This was the first, or front, street on the 1856 plat map. The other names were equally unimaginative, but thankfully none of them remains. Around 1900, the city wished to change the name of Front Avenue to Larpenteur, but the street's residents were adamant in their defense of the original name.

FRONTENAC PLACE: Previously Glenham Avenue, the name was changed in 1940. Frontenac is a place name in several states; in Minnesota the village is on Lake Pepin.

FRY STREET: William and Ann Fry were among the developers of this street in 1875. Fry was born in Germany and came to St. Paul about 1872 where he acted as an insurance agent. He apparently left St. Paul in 1879.

FULHAM STREET: This is another English name applied in 1885. Fulham is a part of London.

FULLER AVENUE: Alpheus G. Fuller (1822-1900) was born in Connecticut. He came to St. Paul around 1850 and built a

well-known hotel named the Fuller House.   In later years he
moved to the first white settlement in South Dakota, at
Sioux Falls.   This street was named for him in 1856.

FULTON STREET: Originally Fourth Street, the name was
changed in 1872 to honor Robert Fulton (1765-1815),
inventor of the steamboat.

FURNESS STREET: This street was named in 1913 from the
title of the plat: Furness Garden Lots. The plat was
named for Marian Furness, the daughter of Governor
Alexander Ramsey who was responsible for the land left in
Ramsey's estate when he died.

G

GABRIEL ROAD: Formerly the driveway to the ten acre estate of Thomas and Gabriel McGuire, this street was added to the city in 1955 when the property was divided among the descendants. The original McGuire house, built in 1913, remains at 2100 Springside Drive.

GALTIER STREET: Originally Oak Street, the name was changed in 1872 to honor Lucien Galtier (1811-1866), a Roman Catholic priest. Born in France, he was ordained in Dubuque, Iowa and subsequently moved to Mendota (then called St. Peter's) in 1840 as a missionary. He soon after built a log chapel near what is today Minnesota Street and Kellogg Boulevard which he dedicated to St. Paul. Thus our city derived its permanent name.

GARFIELD STREET: Previously Green Street, it was renamed in October, 1881 for James A. Garfield, President of the United States who had been assassinated the previous month.

GARY PLACE: This street was named in 1948 for Gary, eldest son of Alexander G. Tankenoff, president of the Hillcrest Development Company which platted this area as Hillcrest Center.

GENESEE STREET: Edmund Rice named this street in 1870 for the county of the same name in western New York state. Genesee is an Iroquois word meaning "valley beautiful."

GEORGE STREET: George W. H. Bell (1812-1900) was the first white man to settle across the river in what is now the West Side of St. Paul. Coming to Minnesota in 1851, he took a claim of 160 acres, which included property between Bancroft and State streets as well as the present-day Riverview Industrial Park. He gradually sold his claim off for building lots as the city grew. This street, one of the first, was named in 1855.

GERANIUM AVENUE: Iglehart, Hall and Mackubin, natives of Maryland, may have had that more temperate climate in mind when naming this street in 1857.

GERMAIN STREET: The first Germain Street was named in 1886. Two years later, the name was shifted two blocks west to its present location. Germain is a French word meaning former resident of Germany. On the original plat, the street name appears to be Germania, the Latin word for Germany. Germania was a popular term at the time; Germain most likely borrows from it.

GIBBS AVENUE: Previously Rich Street, the name was changed in 1888. Heman R. Gibbs (1815-1891), an early pioneer in the area, took a claim for 160 acres in an area today bounded by Cleveland, Fulham, Larpenteur and Roselawn avenues. He moved here in 1849, and built a frame house in 1854, which he greatly enlarged in 1867. That house, which overlooked an Indian trail between Forest Lake and Lake Harriet, remains at 2097 Larpenteur Avenue West, maintained as a museum by the Ramsey County-St. Paul Historical Society.

GILBERT AVENUE: This street was platted in 1887 by Celestia and Newington Gilbert of Washington County, Minnesota.

GLEN ROAD: Glen was a very popular word of the nineteenth century. Celtic in origin, and introduced by the writings of Sir Walter Scott, its specific meaning of a narrow valley is not always observed. This street was named in 1888.

GLEN TERRACE: Part of the Glen Terrace Addition, this street was named in 1912.

GLENDALE STREET: Glen is a popular prefix; dale a popular suffix; both mean valley. This name was applied in 1887.

GLENRIDGE AVENUE: See Berland Place.

GOODHUE STREET: Originally platted as Grove Street in 1849, the name was changed in 1872 to honor James M. Goodhue (1810-1852). He was born in New Hampshire, admitted to the Bar in New York, practiced law in Illinois and Wisconsin before migrating to St. Paul in 1849 where he established the first newspaper in the state. Goodhue was a man of what used to be called "warm temperament" meaning he had a quick temper and strong opinions which made him many enemies and friends; in fact, he was once attacked and stabbed as the result of his journalism. An ardent booster of St. Paul and Minnesota, he exploited every opportunity to promote their growth. A Minnesota county is also named in his honor.

GOODRICH AVENUE: "A walking encyclopedia of ancient and biblical history; an arsenal of fun and fact; a magazine full of argumentative missiles; a volcanic explosion in the midst of the religious element, and a generally accepted electric battery, from which a thousand positive forces penetrate the citadels of bigotry and ignorance." Thus

Hon. AARON GOODRICH
"a volcanic explosion in the midst of the religious element"

reads one description of Aaron Goodrich (1807-1887) for whom this street was named in 1849. Chief Justice of Minnesota Territory, active in the legal organization of the state, he was also a founder of the Republican Party in Minnesota.

GORDON AVENUE: This street name, applied in 1885 as part of St. Anthony Park, is probably that of some investor, but whom I cannot say.

GORMAN AVENUE: Called an "ill-bred, second-rate, barroom politician," Willis A. Gorman (1816-1876) was Governor of Minnesota Territory when this street was named in 1855. Born in Kentucky, he moved to Indiana with his parents, graduated from Law School, was elected to the legislature for several terms and served in the Mexican War. In 1853, President Franklin Pierce appointed him Governor of our Territory, largely because Gorman was in favor of slavery. He was an astute, ruthless, and blustery officeholder who

GOVERNOR WILLIS A. GORMAN
"an ill bred, second rate, bar room politician"

felt the end justified the means. When Gorman was Governor, he and several other legislators, owning large parcels of land near St. Peter, made a determined effort to remove the capitol from St. Paul to that city. They were defeated only when one of the other legislators stole the bill and disappeared with it. On this occasion a disappointed Gorman was heard to remark that he would "live long enough to see grass grow in the streets of St. Paul."

GOTZIAN STREET: Adam and Josephine Gotzian were the developers of this street in 1883. Adam was born in Germany, came to St. Paul in 1860, and engaged with his brother, Conrad, in the boot and shoe trade, but Adam later dabbled in real estate.

GOVE PLACE: Emma B. Gove was Secretary of the St. Paul Mutual Insurance Company, one of the two companies deeding this land to the city in 1937 for use as a street.

GRACE LANE: Theron and Grace B. Anderson lived on Upper Afton Road for many years, and named this street in 1953.

GRACE STREET: Originally platted as College Street in 1856, the name was changed in 1872. The new name was probably suggested by Thomas Grace (1826-1905), a building contractor and mason, who was an alderman and member of the City Council Committee on Streets at the time. However, the name is also said to honor Thomas L. Grace (1814-1897) Roman Catholic Bishop of St. Paul at this time. The western part of Grace Street is now Stanford Avenue.

GRAHAM AVENUE: John A. Graham owned fifty-five acres near the west end of the street in 1891. He is listed as a resident of the city for only one year.

GRAND AVENUE: Grand has two meanings: the English sense of magnificent, sublime, which is common in the eastern United States; and the Spanish sense of large which is common in the Western states. This street was named in 1871 by an Englishman, John Wann.

GRAND HILL: When Oakland Avenue was changed to Grand Avenue in 1970, this portion of Grand Avenue was changed to Grand Hill. The change was at the insistence of the Grand Avenue Business Association which wished to extend Grand Avenue to West Seventh Street.

GRANITE STREET: This street was named in 1870 for the rock; the word suggests permanence, steadfastness, beauty. An intersecting street is called Agate.

GRANTHAM STREET: A village in England, near London, prompted this name in 1885.

GREEN STREET: Joseph C. Green was a real estate partner of Edwin Sargent who platted this street in 1885.   Green died in St. Paul on October 10, 1890, at the age of 73.

GREENBRIER STREET: Greenbrier County in West Virginia was the basis of this 1857 street name.

GREENLAND AVENUE: Originally Wentworth Avenue, the name was changed in 1927.   Fish Creek, one of the few natural streams left within the city limits, flows under Greenland Avenue. The brook takes its name from David Fish, an early settler in McLean Township, who had a farm along Upper Afton Road.

GREENWOOD AVENUE: The name was changed--from B Street to Greenwood Avenue--in 1883.

GRIFFITH STREET: This street was platted by Benjamin Hoyt and John Burns in 1856.   It is most likely a personal name, but whose I cannot say.

GRIGGS STREET: Described by a contemporary as "exceedingly social and pleasant in his nature, yet back of all this he is shrewd and scheming," Chauncey W. Griggs (1832-1910) was a merchant and lumberman who moved to St. Paul in 1856. After serving as a Colonel in the Civil War, he was a state senator and representative, and also invested heavily in real estate, naming this street in 1873.   In 1888, Griggs moved to Tacoma, Washington where he died.

Fountain Cave near St. Paul, looking out.   No. 1508.

GROTTO STREET: Grotto is a synonym for cave.   This street was named in 1871 because, it is said, if the street were extended south it would reach the Mississippi River bank very near Fountain Cave, an early landmark of St. Paul. An historic marker on Shepard Road near Randolph Avenue indicates the location of this cave where "Pigs Eye" Parrant first sold whiskey to the Indians and the soldiers at Fort Snelling.

GROVE STREET: Applied in 1851, this popular name suggests a clump of trees.

GROVELAND STREET: This common name given here in 1888 derives its appeal from the fact that a grove of trees is a pleasant place, especially on the prairies of the Midwest.

GURNEY STREET: Henry B. and Adeline Gurney named this street in 1886 as part of Gurney Park.   Henry, a real estate dealer, died in 1890; Adeline in 1912.

HADLEY STREET: Like many street names in Desnoyer Park which were platted by the Union Land Company in 1888, this one comes from a village in Massachusetts.

HAGUE AVENUE: This street was platted in 1857 by William Holcombe and his son, Edwin, in honor of The Hague, the seat of government of the Netherlands. Holcombe had prominent Dutch ancestors on his maternal side.

HALL AVENUE: Amos W. Hall (1824-   ), was one of the developers of this street in 1855. Born in Massachusetts, he is listed as living in the city as a real estate dealer until 1860.

HAMLINE AVENUE: Leonidas L. Hamline (1797-1865) began his career as an Ohio lawyer. Converted to Methodism in 1829, he spent several years as a circuit rider before his election to Bishop in 1844. Shortly before his death in Iowa, he donated $25,000 to help establish what is now Hamline University. This street was named in 1874 as part of a tract around the school.

HAMMER AVENUE: George H. Hammer was in the real estate business when this street was named in 1886, but he later left St. Paul. His brother, Frederick, became prominent as Mayor Andrew Kiefer's secretary and later served as President of the Board of Public Works in 1900-1902.

HAMPDEN AVENUE: John Hampden (1594-1643), an English political leader, is commemorated in this 1885 street name.

HAMPSHIRE AVENUE: This street was named in 1946 as part of Hampshire Park. English names are always fashionable.

HANCOCK STREET: General Winfield Scott Hancock (1824-1886) was a Presidential candidate when this street was named in 1880 by his friend, Franz Sigel (1824-1902), a fellow general in the Civil War. Sigel, who lived in New York, visited New Ulm and St. Paul in 1873 and invested in property here.

HARDENBERGH PLACE: Although platted in 1886 by Joseph
Lockey, a cashier at the National German American Bank, this
street name is probably that of Peter R. Hardenbergh who
developed another addition to the city in 1887.

HARRISON AVENUE: Originally Prairie Street, the name was
changed in 1889 to avoid duplication. Benjamin Harrison
(1833-1901) was President of the United States at this time.

HARTFORD AVENUE: The city in Connecticut most likely
prompted this name in 1886.

HARVARD STREET: Previously Hancock Street, the name was
changed in 1883. College names were popular in the nineteenth century.

HATCH AVENUE: Edwin A. C. Hatch (1825-1882) is commemorated
by this street named in the year of his death. Born in New
York state, he migrated to Minnesota in 1843 as an Indian
trader. Subsequently an Indian agent to the Blackfoot
tribe, he was also Major of a cavalry battalion during the
Sioux Uprising. It was Hatch who kidnapped two Sioux
Indian chiefs from their refuge in Canada, and returned them
to the United States where they were hanged for their part
in the Indian War.

HATHAWAY STREET: This 1883 street name might have indicated
William Hathaway, a clerk for the nearby railroad.

HAWLEY STREET: Jesse B. Hawley was the surveyor of this
subdivision in 1885.

HAWTHORNE AVENUE: Iglehart, Hall and Mackubin, natives of
Maryland, may have had that more temperate climate in mind
when naming the street in 1857 for this shrub.

HAZEL STREET: Hazel was a common shrub in the area, when
this street was named in 1890 as part of Hazel Park.

HAZELWOOD AVENUE: Platted as Bock Avenue, the name was
changed in 1915. Hazelwood seems more in keeping with
Hazel Park, and has a finer sound to it.

HEATHER DRIVE: Originally Floral Street, location of the
home of Cass Gilbert, noted local architect, the name was
changed at the request of its resident in 1959. The change
was to emphasize its connection with Heather Place, just
adjacent.

HEATHER PLACE: James W. and Alma M. Heather platted this
street in 1889. They were not residents of St. Paul,
although they may have lived within the county.

HENDON AVENUE: This street was named in 1885 for a suburb
of London.

HERBERT STREET: William Hamm named this street in 1887 as part of Hazel Park.

HERSCHEL STREET: Originally Franklin Avenue, the name was changed in 1886 to avoid duplication. Herschel is possibly a first name, but whose I cannot say.

HERSEY STREET: Platted in 1882, east of Hamline Avenue, this street was extended west to its present location, while the name of the eastern portion was changed to Taylor Avenue. The developers were Roscoe (1841-1906) and Eva Hersey, and Edward L. (1856-1908) and Mary Hersey. These two Hersey brothers were born in Maine but moved to Minnesota to manage a lumber business established at Stillwater by their father. Upon his death, the sons inherited the business which was known as Hersey, Staples and Company.

HEWITT AVENUE: Girart Hewitt (1825-1879) was born in Pennsylvania and traveled to St. Paul in 1856 where he opened a real estate office. He conceived the idea of an annual steamboat ride upon the Mississippi River in December which was widely reported in the newspapers, and served to allay the Eastern opinion of our harsh winters. The street was named in 1875.

HIGHLAND PARKWAY: Platted as Otto Street, the name of this portion was changed in 1934. The name Highland is very common, and appears throughout the city. Its use in this neighborhood is suggested by the Highland Spring Water Company established in 1901 at Randolph Avenue and Lexington Parkway, or the hill where the Highland water tower now stands, the highest point of the surrounding region.

HIGHWOOD AVENUE: Giving the impression of height and trees, this 1887 name is pleasant, but trite.

HILDING AVENUE: Hilding Johnson (1898-1974) was the father-in-law of Warren Forsberg, the surveyor of this plat in 1959.

HILL STREET: This street was named in 1849 for the hill it ascends between Eagle Street and Kellogg Boulevard.

HILLCREST AVENUE: Part of St. Catherine Park, this very common name was applied in 1919.

HILLSDALE AVENUE: See Berland Place.

HILLSIDE AVENUE: Previously Langford Avenue, the name was changed in 1940.

HILLTOP LANE: The location prompted this street name in 1948.

HOFFMAN AVENUE: Originally named Dayton Avenue, the name was changed in 1872 to honor James K. Hoffman (1831-1905).

Born in Pennsylvania, he came to St. Paul in 1851, where he
operated three different sawmills, one of which stood at the
bottom of Dayton's Bluff. Hoffman later became a merchant
and a state official; at the time of the name change he was
a member of the City Council.

HOLLY AVENUE: James Burbank, John Merriam and Horace
Thompson, prominent businessmen, named this street in 1870
for the Holly tree, which, because of its sound and Christmas
associations, conveys a pleasant impression.

HOLTON STREET: This street was named in 1881.

HOMER STREET: Previously Purnell Avenue, the name was
changed in 1940.

HOPE STREET: Once Hill Street, the name was changed in 1872.

HOPKINS STREET: Benjamin W. Brunson named this street in
1852 for Daniel Hopkins, a native of New Hampshire who lived
at Prairie du Chien along with the Brunson family from 1838
to 1844. Both Brunson and Hopkins moved to St. Paul in 1847,
but Hopkins died June 13, 1852, a month before this street
was platted.
       Hopkins Street is in one of the most historic areas of
the city. On a spit of land between Phalen Creek and Trout
Brook, the area was first known as Bilanski Point for
Stanislaus Bilanski, an early settler who was murdered by
his wife. In later years, encircled by tracks, it was known
as Railroad Island.

HORACE STREET: Thomas and Louisa Campbell named this street
in 1887 for one of their family.

HORTON AVENUE: Hiler H. Horton (1857-1906) was born in
Wisconsin. Upon graduation from Washington University in
St. Louis he moved to St. Paul in 1878 as a clerk in the
law office of Cushman K. Davis. Horton served on the Board
of Park Commissioners and was later a state Senator. The
proximity of the street to Como Park prompted the use of
his name in 1885.

HOWARD STREET: The Union Land Company named this street in
1887. It is unlikely that it has any special meaning.

HOWELL STREET: Platted as part of Merriam Park in 1882,
the name might be a reference to Samuel L. Howell, a
Philadelphia real estate dealer.

HOYT AVENUE: Lorenzo and Sarah Hoyt platted this street in
1872. He was the son of Benjamin F. Hoyt (1800-1875),
pioneer preacher, for whom the street is said to be named.
Benjamin came to St. Paul in 1848 where he dealt largely in
real estate. It is related that when Lorenzo was breaking

the sod at his farm near today's Hamline and Larpenteur avenues then worth five dollars an acre, and feeling his prospects were poor, his father reassured him: "Well, boys, do not be discouraged; you will live to see this land sell for $50 an acre."

HUBBARD AVENUE: Lucius F. Hubbard (1836-1913) was Governor of Minnesota when this street was named in 1882. Born in New York, he came to Red Wing in 1857 where he established a newspaper. He was active in the Civil War and subsequently entered the grain and flour milling business. Hubbard County is also named in his honor.

HUDSON ROAD: Previously Hastings Avenue, the name was changed in 1940, for Hudson, Wisconsin, the destination of the street.

HUMBOLDT AVENUE: Originally Goff Avenue, the name, changed in 1916, is taken from Humboldt High School, built on this street in 1910. The school, second of that name, commemorates Alexander von Humboldt (1769-1859), a German naturalist and explorer, one of the earliest and most influential scientists.

HUNT PLACE: This street was named in 1885 as part of St. Anthony Park, for Daniel H. Hunt (1833-1891) and his wife, Annie Lockwood Hunt (1846-1932) who owned a farm in the area today roughly east of Highway 280, between Ellis and Pearl streets. Hunt moved here from Maine in 1857, married Annie Lockwood, and after fighting in the Civil War, purchased the Lockwood farm in 1870. He was a truck farmer selling his produce in the Twin Cities. The Hunt farmhouse at 2478 Territorial Road was built in 1874 and demolished in 1973 by the Stockwell Equipment Company.

HUNTING VALLEY ROAD: The St. Paul City Council named this street in 1960 at the request of the Quality Park Envelope Company, 2520 Como Avenue. At the time, the company was planning a promotion for which they wished to use a different mailing address to their same building. They therefore had the street alongside their building changed to Hunting Valley Road, and they named their promotion firm The Valley Envelope Company. For a frontage road on a freeway, the name is incongruous, to say the least.

HURON STREET: Part of Chelsea Heights, this street was named in 1916 presumably for the Indian tribe in the eastern United States. The exact significance of the name, if any, is not recalled.

HYACINTH AVENUE: Iglehart, Hall and Mackubin, natives of Maryland, may have had that more temperate climate in mind when naming this street in 1857.

HYTHE STREET: Hythe is a village in Kent County, England, near Dover. This street was named in 1885.

I

IDAHO AVENUE: This street was named in 1886, like the potato, for the western state.

IGLEHART AVENUE: Remembered as "gentlemanly and courteous in his bearing, kind and considerate," Harwood Iglehart (1829-1893) was born in Maryland and received his law degree from Harvard University. After practicing law in Annapolis for a short time, he moved to St. Paul in 1854. While continuing his profession here, he dealt heavily in real estate, and made several additions to the city, including this one in 1855. Iglehart served as president of the Mercantile Library Association, on the first Board of Trustees for St. Luke's Hospital and in numerous other civic posts. It was Iglehart's firm conviction that St. Paul and Minneapolis would soon join together and become one large city.

IOWA AVENUE: In 1886, this street was named for the state following a precedent set in Washington, D.C.

IRIS PLACE: Lake Iris, a small artificial pond nearby, prompted this street name in 1888.

IROQUOIS AVENUE: Part of Beaver Lake Heights, this street was named in 1917 for the Iroquois, a confederation of several eastern Indian tribes.

IRVINE AVENUE: "A man of the people; a man of no ostentation; a laborer, always working; never idle; quiet in manners; strictly temperate, and very even in his everyday toil," John R. Irvine (1812-1878) was born in Dansville, New York. He traveled to St. Paul in the winter of 1843 when he bought about 300 acres (at a dollar an acre) east and north of Wabasha Avenue--now among the most valuable property in the city.

IRVINE PARK AVENUE: In 1876, the St. Paul City Council designated the street around Irvine Park as Irvine Park Avenue. The name is that of John R. Irvine (1812-1878) who gave the public square to the city in 1849.

ISABEL STREET: This street was named about 1855, for whom
I do not know.

ITASCA AVENUE: Originally Coburn Avenue, the name was
changed in 1940.

IVAN WAY: Ivan J. and Catherine Kipp were the developers
of this addition in 1912; they moved to Los Angeles in
1925.

IVY AVENUE: Iglehart, Hall and Mackubin, natives of
Maryland, may have had that more temperate climate in mind
when naming this street in 1857.

J

JACKSON STREET: "A short, thick-set man, slow in speech, quiet in his movements, with a florid complexion, and a mouth full of tobacco" -- such is the description of Henry Jackson (1811-1857), one of the earliest settlers of St. Paul. Born in Virginia, Jackson went to Texas, and then drifted to New York, Wisconsin, Illinois, and finally Minnesota. He settled in St. Paul in 1842 where he established a general store and acted as the first postmaster. One of the first streets of the city, platted in 1849, Jackson Street was one of the main commercial thoroughfares of St. Paul and possessed, at its foot, one of the city's two steamboat landings.

JAMES AVENUE: James Stinson (1828-1917), one of the developers, named this street in 1854. Born in Hamilton, Ontario, later a resident of Chicago, Stinson made twenty-four additions to the city of St. Paul, was one of the founders of Superior, Wisconsin, and invested heavily in Chicago canal lands. A quiet, reserved man of immense wealth, he was probably the largest land owner in Ramsey County during the nineteenth century. Thomas Street is named for his father, and Stinson Street and Stinson Boulevard are also named for him.

JAMESON STREET: Frank and Carrie Crowell named this street in 1907.

JANET STREET: The titian-haired editor of this tome inspired the name of this ghost street. Reflective and perceptive by nature, she is also known variously as a buoyant bibliophile, a creature of engaging manner, and the possessor of an impish, pungent wit.

JAYNE STREET: This street was named in 1951 for the daughter of Herbert West, Plat Commissioner at the time.

JEFFERSON AVENUE: Thomas Jefferson, third President of the United States, is commemorated in this 1854 street name. He was related to the prominent Randolph family of Virginia.

JENKS AVENUE: Recalled as "a quiet, retiring man in his disposition, a gentleman of uniform habits and a good citizen," Jonathan R. Jenks (1832?-1890) was born in Pennsylvania. He moved to St. Paul in 1855 to be with his brother-in-law, Governor Alexander Ramsey, and entered the drug business with Dr. David Day. A subsequent drug store went bankrupt, and Jenks spent the remainder of his life as a clerk with the War Department at Fort Snelling.

Jenks Drug Store at Kellogg Boulevard and Cedar Street circa 1875.

JESSAMINE AVENUE: Iglehart, Hall and Mackubin, natives of Maryland, may have had that more temperate climate in mind when naming this street in 1857.

JESSIE STREET: Jessie Rice (1851-1874) was the second daughter of Edmund Rice, the developer of this street in 1855. Jessie married Frank H. Clark of Philadelphia who had come to St. Paul briefly as President of the Lake Superior and Mississippi Railroad Company.

JOHN STREET: When named in 1852, this street was assigned the most common of all male names. John Baptiste Coty, one of the original proprietors of St. Paul was a man of some standing and property in the early times of the city, but, it is recorded, the infidelity of his wife with a prominent citizen so unsettled him that he returned to his native Canada where he died.

JOHN IRELAND BOULEVARD: This new boulevard was named in 1961 for John Ireland (1838-1918), Roman Catholic Archbishop of St. Paul from 1884 until his death. Born in Ireland, he immigrated to St. Paul in 1853 with his parents.

FATHER JOHN IRELAND
"The fighting chaplain"

An appealing, intellectual boy, he was sent to France by
Bishop Cretin where he was educated as a priest. Returning
to St. Paul, he enlisted in the Civil War where he earned
fame as a fighting chaplain. After the war, he actively
entered the civic life of the city, speaking out against
political corruption and the liquor interests. He also
became involved in moving immigrants from the crowded cities
of the East to western Minnesota where he established immigrant colonies. Patriotic in his public speech, active in
promoting the interests of the church and state, he established a parochial school system throughout the Archdiocese,
including the institutions of St. Thomas College, St. Paul
Seminary, and, with his sister, St. Catherine's College.
He was responsible for the platting of Groveland as well as
the building of the St. Paul Cathedral and the Basilica of
St. Mary's in Minneapolis. Ireland was tri-lingual, inter-
nationally known, liberal for his day, and one of the
greatest spokesmen for the American Catholic Church as well
as one of the builders of St. Paul.

JOHNSON PARKWAY: The original street in this location,
named Johnson Street in 1856, was probably in honor of
Gates A. Johnson (1826-1918), a surveyor and civil engineer.
Born in New York, Gates moved to St. Paul in 1855 where he
was subsequently chief engineer for one of the railroads.
     The street was later expanded into Johnson Parkway.
Stretching between Indian Mounds Park and Phalen Park, this
more recent name commemorated John A. Johnson (1861-1909),
Governor of Minnesota from 1905-1909.

*Looking north on Johnson Parkway from Bush Avenue. Two
of the houses in the background remain at 852 and 862
Johnson Parkway.*

JONES STREET: Edwin F. Jones (1896-1961) was city utilities engineer when this street was named by the City Council in 1956.   Born in St. Paul, he grew up in North Dakota, returning to graduate from the University of Minnesota in 1916. After the war, he opened an engineering office, but subsequently went to work for the city in 1922 where he served as an engineer on the construction of the Auditorium.   In his later years with the city, he was considered an expert on public utility rates.

JORDAN AVENUE: This street was named in 1917 for James W. Jordan, chief clerk of the Department of Public Works.   He was born July 4, 1863 in St. Paul of Irish parents and died August 12, 1934.

JOSEPHINE PLACE: Platted in 1886 as part of the Henry Herrn farm (one of the pioneers of Reserve Township), this street was later extended south.

JOY AVENUE: Charles and Jane Joy of St. Paul named this street in 1884.

JUDSON AVENUE: Familiarly known as "Carl," Roswell Carlton Judson (1844-1905) was born in Chenango County, New York. After the Civil War, he moved to Farmington in Dakota County, his home when he was elected Secretary of the Minnesota State Agricultural Society, the organization responsible for the State Fair and the naming of this street within the Fairgrounds.   It was during his term as Secretary, in 1885, that the State Fair, having been held in Rochester, Owatonna, and other cities around the state, purchased their permanent home at the suburb of Hamline, a location deliberately chosen to avoid the appearance of prejudice toward either St. Paul or Minneapolis.

JULIET AVENUE: William and Nell Nettleton and their son, George, owned a 130 acre dairy farm in the vicinity of Randolph Avenue and Lexington Parkway.   William had a daughter, Julia; the diminutive of this name is Juliet, a street name applied by the family in 1886.

JUNIPER LANE: Named by the City Council in 1967, this is one of the streets within Highland Park.   The name is derived from some juniper bushes planted along this route.

JUNO AVENUE: In 1880 gold was discovered in Alaska; the following year the miners attracted to the site organized a town and called it Juneau for one of their members.   This street was named in 1881, either as a misspelling (intentional or otherwise) or for the Goddess, Juno.

K

KANSAS AVENUE: Originally Hoyt Avenue, the present name
is that of the state.

KASOTA AVENUE: Previously Wheeler Street, the name was
changed in 1940 to avoid duplication.

KAUFMAN DRIVE: Named by the City Council in 1967, this is
one of the streets within Como Park. W. LaMont Kaufman
(1894-1971) was Superintendent of Parks in St. Paul from
1932 to 1965. Born in Belmond, Iowa, he moved to St. Paul
in 1919 as a landscape architect.

KELLOGG BOULEVARD: Probably no other street name in the
history of the city commanded as much attention and
publicity as the naming of Kellogg Boulevard. The street
was originally platted as Third Street and it was the main
business thoroughfare up into the 1880's when it began to
lose its appeal. The businesses along the street became
progressively more shabby and dirty, as did their buildings,
occupants, and customers. In 1927 the city began a massive
renewal project which included clearing out most of the
buildings on the south side of the street, thus making
available a view of the river which had been lacking since
the earliest days of the city. In order to dispel the
image of old Third Street, the St. Paul Pioneer Press-
Dispatch and the St. Paul Real Estate Board held a contest
for the selection of another name. The winner of the $100
prize was Albert Slawik, a theatre organist in St. Paul.
     Frank B. Kellogg (1856-1937), lawyer, Senator, and
United States Secretary of State, was considered St. Paul's
leading citizen at the time. Born in New York, he moved
with his family to a farm in southern Minnesota directly
after the Civil War. Despite a sketchy education, he was
admitted to the Bar in 1877 and subsequently became associated with Cushman K. Davis, Minnesota's leading lawyer.
However, Kellogg soon departed from his corporate law
pattern, and led the federal prosecution of some major
monopolies, including the Standard Oil Trust. With the
attention garnered from these national law cases, he became
President of the American Bar Association, and subsequently

Construction involved in the dramatic transition from Third Street to Kellogg Boulevard.

United States Senator. After World War I, he served as
Ambassador to Great Britain and was later (1925) appointed
United States Secretary of State. His house in St. Paul, in
which he lived intermittently from 1889 to 1937, still stands
at 633 Fairmount Avenue.

The naming of this street on December 20, 1932 was the
occasion of a great celebration, with fireworks, a parade,
and thousands in attendance. The City Council met in special
session on the stage of the Auditorium for the sole purpose
of bestowing this new name.

KENNARD STREET: Kennard Buxton was the attorney for the
developer, Joseph Lee, in 1878. Buxton was not a local
resident.

KENNETH STREET: Eugene Underwood (1818-1893) and his wife,
Fredericka, of Louisville, Kentucky platted this street in
1887. They owned considerable property in Groveland Park,
and at one time Wheeler Street was Fredericka Street and
Davern Street was Underwood Street. Eugene came from a
prominent Kentucky family but lived in St. Paul from 1865
to 1875, where he was a distinguished lawyer. His son,
Oscar W. Underwood was a candidate for the Democratic
nomination for President in 1912.

KENNY ROAD: Originally named Patridge Street in the 1850's,
the street name was changed in 1960 because the Kenny Boiler
and Manufacturing Company moved to a new site on this street.
The company, a St. Paul industry, was founded by John and
Terence Kenny in 1869, soon after the first railroad came to
Minnesota. John's sons, Louis T. (1887-1970) and Phillip J.
(1894-1973) managed the company from the early 1900's until
it passed out of the family in 1965.

KENT STREET: This street was named in 1855 by Charles
Mackubin from Maryland for Kent County in that state.

KENTUCKY STREET: Previously Fourth Street, the name was
changed in 1876 to commemorate the state.

KENWOOD PARKWAY: Originally Kenwood Terrace, the name was
changed in 1888. The surrounding area is known as Kenwood
Park, a popular name which originated with Kenwood, Illinois,
a Chicago suburb.

KESTON STREET: The village in England prompted this street
name in 1885.

KILBURN STREET: Kilburn is a part of London, England,
northwest of St. Paul's Cathedral. The street was named in
1885 when English names were especially popular.

KING STREET: This street was platted in 1857 by, among others,
David H. King (1829?-   ). Born in Connecticut, he traveled

to St. Paul in 1857 with his family and brother, Henry J.
King. Both are recorded as lumber merchants and both had
left the state by 1860.

KINGSFORD STREET: Once Balsam Street, the name was changed
in 1947. Walter J. Kingsford (1874-1946) was manager of
Twin City Hamline Realty, the company developing the property. Born in Rushford, Minnesota, Kingsford taught in
the rural schools for five years before moving to St. Paul
in 1908, where he entered the real estate business, later
becoming President of the Minnesota Realty Association.
His widow remembers this plat bearing his name as a large
swamp which had to be filled in.

KIPLING STREET: See Berland Place.

*Norman Kittson's $100,000 Victorian mansion on the site of the present
Cathedral. It was rumored that, because of a superstitious foreboding,
Kittson never slept overnight in his palatial home.*

KITTSON STREET: Considered unassuming and undemonstrative
in his manners, quiet and unobtrusive, and very reticent
in business matters, Norman W. Kittson (1814-1888) was
ranked as one of the richest men in the Northwest. Born in
Canada, he came to Minnesota as a sutler at Fort Snelling

in 1834. He next worked as an independent fur trader,
established steamboat transportation on the Red River, and
invested heavily in railroads with James J. Hill. He was
elected to the state legislature and served a term as Mayor
of St. Paul. In his later years, "Commodore" Kittson spent
much of his time in New York City. When asked why, he
replied that in St. Paul he was constantly pestered by people
who were trying to get at his money bags. This street was
named in 1854.

KLAINERT STREET: This street was added to the city in 1950
as part of the McDonough public housing project. Robert
John Klainert (1924-1945) was a serviceman killed in action
in Germany during World War II. His name was suggested by
the Nels Wold (#5) Chapter of the Military Order of the
Purple Heart because both Robert and his father, Joseph,
were recipients of the Purple Heart award. John J. McDonough
(1895-1962), for whom the housing project was named, was
Mayor of St. Paul from 1940-1948.

KNAPP STREET: John H. (1825-1888) and Nellie Knapp were two
of the developers of this street in 1885. Knapp was born in
Elmira, New York, traveled to Iowa about the age of eight
and, in 1846, moved to the site of Menomonie, Wisconsin
where he bought an interest in a sawmill. The business
increased tremendously until, in the 1880's, under the name
Knapp, Stout Lumber Company, it was considered the largest
lumbering concern in the world. Knapp was an investor in
St. Anthony Park, but never lived in Minnesota.

LAMBERT LANDING (March 1938) A view of the municipal boat-landing
from the Robert Street Bridge.

L

LACROSSE AVENUE: William and Helen Ames, the proprietors of Hazel Park, named this street in 1886. There is a Mississippi river city in Wisconsin by that name.

LAFAYETTE ROAD: In 1872 the City Council combined the three streets of Jefferson, Chestnut, and Herkimer under the name Lafayette, in honor of the Marquis de Lafayette (1757-1834), French statesman and soldier. Thomas Jefferson once described Lafayette as having "a canine appetite for popularity and fame."

LAFOND AVENUE: Benjamin LaFond (1819-1904) platted this street in 1857. He was born in St. Boniface, Canada and moved to St. Paul in 1851 where he dealt in real estate with Auguste Larpenteur and Alexander Ramsey. His numerous descendants still live within the city.

LAKE STREET: This street was named in 1946 for its proximity to Beaver Lake.

LAKEVIEW AVENUE: The street's location near Como Lake prompted this name in 1915.

LAMBERT LANDING: Occupying the site of the first steamboat landing in St. Paul, Lambert Landing was constructed in the 1930's. It was officially named in 1937 for Colonel George C. Lambert (1867-1934) who was a prominent St. Paul attorney and businessman, and a leader in the campaign for a nine-foot navigation channel in the Mississippi River. Born in Belgium, Lambert immigrated to St. Paul in 1887 by way of Ghent, Minnesota. Here he practiced law, served as Adjutant General for a time, grew mushrooms, and was active in the organization of the Farmers Union Terminal Association.

LAMPREY AVENUE: Uri Locke Lamprey (1842-1906) was a prominent lawyer when this street was named in 1887. He was later active in the establishment of the Minnesota Game and Fish Commission, and served for many years as its President. His wife was a daughter of Louis Robert, for whom Robert Street was named.

LANE PLACE: Both this street and the park nearby were named in 1916 for Den E. Lane, prominent real estate developer.

LANGFORD PARK: Nathaniel P. Langford (1832-1911) and his second wife, Clara were two of the developers of this street in 1885. Born in upstate New York, Langford came to St. Paul in 1854, where he worked in banking. In the 1860's he was Collector of Internal Revenue in Montana during the gold rush days. Organizer of an expedition that discovered the Yellowstone geysers, he became the first superintendent of Yellowstone Park. He wrote two books about his experiences in the West. In St. Paul he was the primary organizer of the investors for St. Anthony Park and much of today's Como Avenue, as it runs through St. Anthony Park, was formerly Langford Avenue. Langford died one of St. Paul's most colorful and respected citizens.

LARCH STREET: The larch is a common North American tree better known as tamarack, which is a common species in this area. All the adjacent streets, most of which have been renamed, also bore tree names. This street was platted in 1856.

LARPENTEUR AVENUE: Originally Minneapolis Avenue, the name was changed by the City Council in 1904. Auguste L. Larpenteur (1823-1919) was born in Baltimore, grandson of a French emigre. As a young man, he moved to St. Louis, and subsequently to St. Paul in 1843 as one of its first twelve settlers. He helped lay out the original city and claimed 160 acres in the Midway, near Lexington Parkway and University Avenue, which he sold to his Uncle Eugene who farmed it. Engaged in the fur trading and merchandising business, Larpenteur built his family home in 1860 near what is today Dale Street and Interstate 94, and called it the "Anchorage." He spoke French, English, and several Indian languages; he moved, thought, and acted quickly, and was well regarded by all who knew him. In the later years of his life, he was the oldest living settler in St. Paul, and it was for this reason the street was renamed in his honor.

LARRY HO DRIVE: Larry Ho was the pen name of Laurence Curran Hodgson (1874-1937) Mayor of St. Paul 1918-1922, 1926-1930. Born in Hastings, he began work, at fourteen, as a printer's devil on the newspaper Hastings Democrat, working his way up to the staff of the Minneapolis Tribune by 1897. In subsequent years, he held several posts within state government and served as a writer for the St. Paul newspapers. After his terms as Mayor, he wrote a regular column for the St. Paul Dispatch. A prolific writer, an entertaining speaker, he had a great faculty for making friends. Part of his creed, written in 1935, is:
       "If I die tonight, I should wish men to say of me:
'He was a sort of foolish fellow, but he never failed when

AUGUSTE L. LARPENTEUR
"Grandfather of the City"

we needed him. His brain may have been wabbly, but his
heart was staunch. He was our friend.'"
    Upon his death, Hodgson's body lay in state at the
foot of the giant Indian in the concourse of the City Hall.
This street was named by the City Council in 1959.

LaSALLE STREET: This street was named in 1881 for Sieur
de LaSalle (1643-1687), French explorer. This name was
selected, no doubt, because of its sound.

LAUREL AVENUE: Like Ashland and Holly avenues, this street
was named for the tree in 1870. The classical use of the
leaves as a crown of victory makes this an attractive name.

LAVAL STREET: This street was named for the French town
where one of St. Paul's erstwhile citizens, James Taylor
Dunn, was briefly stationed during World War II.

LAWSON AVENUE: This street was named in 1872, most likely
in honor of some individual, but whom I cannot say.

LAWTON STREET: Dr. George O. Lawton (1848-1909), a dentist,
owned considerable property in St. Paul and named this street
in 1871. His house stood on the corner of Grand Hill and
Lawton Street. The "Lawton Steps" descend the hill from
Lawton Street to Grand Avenue.

LEE AVENUE: Another father-son combination is honored in the
naming of this street within the State Fairgrounds. William
Edwin Lee (1852-1920) of Long Prairie was a member of the
Board of Managers of the Minnesota State Agricultural Society
from 1903 to 1909. His son, Raymond A. Lee (1880-1956) was
Secretary of the Society from 1930 to 1950. Raymond's dual
occupations of banker and dealer in farm equipment gave him
a close association with the problems of rural living, and
his knowledge of finance and economics greatly benefited the
Fair during this period of extensive development.

LEECH STREET: Samuel Leech, the developer, was appointed
receiver of the United States Land Office at St. Croix Falls,
Wisconsin, in 1848. He invested heavily in Minnesota land,
and named this street in 1849. Subsequently Land Officer at
Quincy, Illinois, he served there until his death in 1861.

LELAND STREET: Previously Parmer Street, the name was
changed in 1940.

LENOX AVENUE: Lenox is a town in Massachusetts and one of
the most fashionable of the New England resorts. The name
was applied in 1887 by the Union Land Company.

LEONE AVENUE: Leone was the wife of Grege Beckett, Plat
Commissioner when this street was named in 1960. Mrs.
Beckett has been a St. Paul school teacher for many years.

LEVEE ROAD: Named by the City Council in 1964, this is the road running along the top of the dike from Wabasha Avenue to Water Street, and from Water Street to Navy Island. Levee is a synonym for dike.

LEXINGTON PARKWAY: John Wann, an Englishman, named this street in 1871 at the instigation of his wife, an American. She felt some redress was needed for the many British street names (Avon, Oxford, Milton), so she suggested this name in honor of the Battle of Lexington in 1775, the first battle of the American Revolution--in which the British were defeated.

In 1907, an attempt was made to change the name to Wheelock Parkway, but it was blocked by patriotic organizations such as the Daughters of the American Revolution.

According to William Hoyt, an early settler in the area, the street was once a Sioux Indian trail from Little Crow's village at Kaposia (near South St. Paul) to Lakes Josephine and Johanna and on up north. In the 1850's, hundreds of Indians traveled this route on their annual rice gathering expeditions.

LIGGETT STREET: Dean of the Agricultural School and Director of the State Experiment Station from 1888-1909, "Colonel" William M. Liggett (1846-1909) was involved in the management of the Minnesota State Agricultural Society (who named this street within the State Fairgrounds) from 1890 until his death. A resident of Benson, Minnesota, Liggett was an experienced and successful cattle breeder, an expertise he brought to the State Fair. It was during Liggett's term as Manager, in 1899, that the first of the night entertainments were scheduled, including a fireworks exhibition entitled "The Burning of Manila."

LIGHTNER PLACE: Elias and Caroline Drake named this street in 1882 for their friend, and later son-in-law, William H. Lightner (1856-1936). He was born in Pennsylvania, graduated from the University of Michigan, traveled to St. Paul in 1878, and was admitted to the Bar as a lawyer in 1880. In 1885 he married Carrie Drake. Lightner later served as a City Councilman, and was generally active in civic affairs.

LINCOLN AVENUE: This street was named in 1871 for Abraham Lincoln. Other streets in the plat were Washington and Madison.

LINDEN STREET: This street was named in 1856 for the tree which is also known as a bass.

LINDER COURT: Willard G. Linder was the trustee of an estate involved in the financing of this development in 1956.

LINWOOD AVENUE: Originally Evergreen Avenue, the name was changed in 1895. Linwood takes its name from the basswood tree, the American linden.

LITCHFIELD STREET: The Litchfield family was active in building the St. Paul and Pacific Railroad. One member of the family, William B. Litchfield, was general manager of the railroad, and a City Councilman. The village in Meeker County, which takes its name from the same family, was also named in 1872.

LITTLE CANADA ROAD: There were several Little Canada Roads. This present one is the remnant of a Civil War road leading north out of St. Paul, along the course of Brainerd Avenue and Edgerton Street, where it swung diagonally northwest to Little Canada, passing close to Wheelock School.

LIVINGSTON AVENUE: Named about 1855, Livingston was, I presume, the middle name of John L. Stryker, a New York state investor on the West Side.

LOEB STREET: The Louis S. and Samuel Loeb real estate company of Duluth platted this street in 1907. The lake nearby took its name from the street; in earlier times, however, the lake was known variously as Dead Horse Lake and Nigger Lake, descriptive names which defy precise explanation.

LOMBARD AVENUE: Lombard is the principal street in London for banks and note brokers, hence it is a synonym for the money market of London, and by extension, it signifies money and capitalism. It was named in 1887.

LONDIN LANE: Previously part of Lower Afton Road, the name was changed in 1963. Robert Londin was a local developer.

LONG AVENUE: Originally Sidney Street, the name was changed in 1886. Long is most likely a personal name, but whose I cannot say.

LONGFELLOW AVENUE: See Berland Place.

L'ORIENT STREET: This is the French word for "east," applied in 1857 because this street was the eastern boundary of that plat. There were many French Canadians in the city at this time.

LOUIS STREET: Joseph Rondo named this street in 1857 for his oldest son, Louis (1835-1913). Joseph Rondo (or Rondeau) was born in Canada, worked as a voyageur and later took up farming near Fort Snelling. When he had to abandon the military reservation, he occupied a small farm near Seven Corners; in 1862 he purchased a large tract of land northeast of the Cathedral, much of which was swamp at the time. Louis, later killed in a train accident, lived at Centerville until 1893 when he moved to Mounds View.

LOUISE AVENUE: Louise is the young-
est daughter of Hyman J. Goldberg
who was, when this street was named
in 1953, office engineer in the
Department of Public Works.

LOWELL STREET: Originally Madison
Street, the name was changed in
1883. Lowell is a common personal
and place name.

LOWER AFTON ROAD: After climbing
the hill from the St. Paul-Point
Douglas Road (now Highway 61), this
early road, built before the Civil
War, ran east into Woodbury Township where it intersected a second
road from St. Paul; both continued
into Afton.

DEN E. LANE
"The Own Your Home Man"

LOWER ST. DENNIS ROAD: Den E. Lane
(1881-1952) was one of the most
active St. Paul real estate men in
the 1920's and 1930's, and a leading
developer of Highland Park. Born in
Ireland, he came to St. Paul as a
child, and began his real estate
ventures while yet a student at St.
Thomas College. Known as the "Own
Your Home Man," Lane estimated that
in the 1920's he had designed, laid
out, and named 50 percent of the St.
Paul streets platted in the preceding decade. By 1925, he had
handled more than ten thousand
property transactions. This street, in 1945, was named for
his patron saint, Dennis.

LUDLOW AVENUE: Previously Nourse Street, the name was
changed in 1940.

LUELLA STREET: Angier and Luella B. Ames of Minneapolis
were relatives of William L. Ames, Jr. who platted Hazel
Park. Luella Ames (1861-1915) was born at Union, Maine
and came to Minneapolis after the Civil War. Upon graduation from Central High and St. Cloud Normal School, she
began a thirty-three year career of teaching in the
Minneapolis Public Schools, including terms as principals
of Kenwood, Humboldt, and Harrison schools. She was well
liked and respected; her death was reported on the front
page of the Minneapolis Journal. This street was named
in 1890.

LUTHER PLACE: Previously Grantham Street, the name was
changed in 1938 for the street's proximity to Luther
Seminary.

LYNNHURST AVENUE: Chosen in 1884, this street name, like
the others in Union Park, was almost surely selected for
its pleasing and somewhat exotic sound. Lynn comes from
the Linden tree; hurst is an old English suffix, revived
in the nineteenth century, meaning wooded hill.

LYON STREET: Herbert Lyon was Director of Civil Service
when this street was opened by the city in 1960.

LYTON PLACE: This property was purchased by Catherine and
Michael Lyton, from Ireland, in 1856. They lived on the
land, and ran a small truck farm. In 1883, the property
was platted, and Lyton's name applied to the street. He
is listed as a resident of the city, under the spelling
Lyden and Lydon until 1891. Descendants of the family
still live in the area.

M

MACALESTER STREET: Platted in 1883, the street took its name from the College, which is named after Charles Macalester (1798-1873), a Philadelphia financier. Edward D. Neill, a fellow Philadelphian, wrote and requested financial aid for the College which Macalester provided in his will. In consideration of this bequest, the name was changed from Baldwin College to Macalester College.

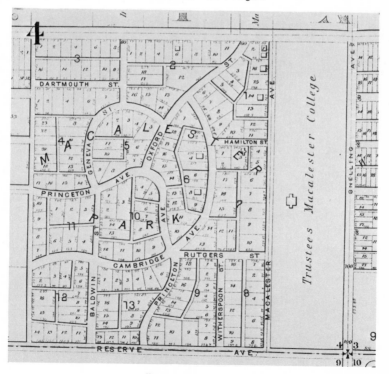

"TANGLETOWN"

Macalester Park as it was originally laid out--before Grand Avenue was put through.

MACKUBIN STREET: Remembered as having "a fine face, indicating good blood," Charles N. Mackubin (1820?-1863) was the developer of this street in 1855. A well-to-do gentleman from Maryland who always wore gold spectacles, Mackubin moved to St. Paul in 1854 where he invested heavily in real estate and banking. The 1860 Census lists his property holdings at $300,000, and a household with three servants and a coachman.

McAFEE STREET: This area was platted in 1885 by the Pioneer Real Estate and Building Society. The streets were named for officers of the Society who were Keller, Johnston, Fisher, Flint, and McAfee. The only name unchanged is for Hugh J. McAfee (1848-1895). He was treasurer of the Society at the time, and the owner of a large foundry and machine shop on Sibley Street.

McBOAL STREET: Described by an early resident as "one of the best and laziest mortals that ever lived," James McClellan Boal (1805?-1862) came to Fort Snelling as a drummer boy under Colonel Leavenworth. He settled in St. Paul in 1846 where he worked as an artist, was subsequently appointed Adjutant General of Minnesota and served in the state legislature. This name, applied to the street in 1849, was Boal's nickname.

McGUIRE LANE: This street was named in 1926 for Thomas and Gabriel McGuire who had a farm and twelve children in the immediate vicinity. The original McGuire house, built in 1913, remains at 2100 Springside Drive.

McKINLEY STREET: William McKinley was President of the United States from 1896 until his assassination in 1901. This street was named in his honor in 1913.

McKNIGHT ROAD: Originally called East Avenue, the name was changed by the City Council in 1957 to honor William L. McKnight (1888-   ), a chief executive of the 3M Company which has its main offices just east of this street. Born on a farm in Brookings County, South Dakota, McKnight, disliking farm work, went to business school in Duluth. Upon graduation, he went to work for the Minnesota Mining and Manufacturing Company (3M) as assistant bookkeeper. Having considerable enthusiasm for the company, he was rapidly promoted to general manager. By 1929, he was President of the company; in 1949, he became Chairman of the Board.

McLEAN AVENUE: At the age of sixty, Nathaniel McLean (1787-1871) abandoned his newspaper business in Ohio and moved to St. Paul. Shortly after his arrival here, he was appointed Sioux Indian agent at Fort Snelling. In 1855, he was elected a Ramsey County Commissioner, and three years later the Dayton's Bluff area was organized into a township and named in his honor. McLean Avenue was named in 1856.

MADISON STREET: Charles A. B. Weide, the developer, lived in Madison, Indiana, for a while before he platted this street in 1872.

MAGNOLIA AVENUE: Iglehart, Hall and Mackubin, natives of Maryland, may have had that more temperate climate in mind when naming this street in 1857.

MAGOFFIN AVENUE: This street was named in 1890 as part of Hiawatha Park for Samuel and Beriah Magoffin. Born in Kentucky, sons of the Civil War governor of that state, they came to St. Paul in the 1880's where they, like the other Kentuckians, Rhodes B. Rankin and Eugene Underwood, invested heavily in Highland Park real estate. Beriah (1843-   ) farmed for a time, was a state legislator for one term and later left the city. Samuel (1859-1934) was a lawyer in St. Paul throughout most of his life. One of Samuel's daughters became the Princess Ibain-Khan Kaplanoff.

MAIDEN LANE: A tiny street, really an alley, made necessary by the topography of the land. Platted in 1854, it most likely takes its name from a narrow street in London, famous as the home of Voltaire.

MAILAND ROAD: Opened by the city in 1917, the road passed through the farm of Julius C. Mailand.

MAIN STREET: Originally part of Fort Street, this street's name was changed by the City Council in 1906.

MANITOBA AVENUE: The "dean of St. Paul real estate men," Robert P. Lewis (1835-1934) came to St. Paul from Penn- sylvania in 1859 as a law school graduate. After the Civil War, he went into real estate, naming this street in 1882.

MANITOU AVENUE: This is the Algonquin Indian word referring to the mysterious and unknown powers of life and of the universe. The street was named in 1917.

MANOMIN AVENUE: This street was named in 1855 as the Chippewa Indian word for wild rice, one of the staples of their diet. There is also a county by this name in Minnesota

MANTON STREET: This street was named in 1891 as part of Manton Park, by Stendal and Maria Manton. A resident of the city from 1891 to 1910, he was a music teacher on the East Side.

MANVEL STREET: Allen Manvel of St. Paul was general manager of the St. Paul, Minneapolis and Manitoba Railway whose tracks ran through St. Anthony Park close to this street. After applying this street name in 1885, Manvel moved to Chicago in 1891.

MAPLE STREET: This street was named in 1857 for the tree.

MARGARET STREET: Previously Pearl Street, the name was changed in 1872. Margaret is derived from the Latin for pearl.

MARIA AVENUE: Lyman Dayton named this street in 1857 for his wife, Maria Bates. Born about 1811, she was a native of Rhode Island. After her husband's death in 1865, she moved to Dayton in Hennepin County. The street name is pronounced "Mah-rye-ah."

MARILLAC LANE: St. Louise DeMarillac (1591-1660) is the inspiration for this 1954 street name. Born in Paris, she was widowed early in life, whereupon she began devoting her time and efforts to helping the needy. When other women began assisting her, she established, with the aid of St. Vincent dePaul, a set of rules for living, and the group took the name: Sisters of Charity of St. Vincent dePaul. St. Louise was canonized in 1934 and declared the patron saint of social workers in 1960. The developer of this street, a widow herself, had a relative in the Sisters of Charity.

MARION STREET: Designated in 1855, the exact significance of this name is obscure. It may be a personal name or more likely it may honor Francis Marion (1732-1795), "the swamp fox," a general in the Revolutionary War, and an epic figure in the nineteenth century. Another early plat (1852) shows a Marion Island in the Mississippi River just off the entrance to Phalen's creek.

MARKET STREET: Because it ran by "Market Square," now known as Rice Park, this street name was applied in 1849. Mears, Rice, and Irvine Parks were all platted as public squares, a piece of undeveloped land; the concept of them as parks, which we have today, did not develop until the 1880's.

MARSH COURT: Charles Marsh, of the Minneapolis real estate and insurance firm of Marsh and Bartlett, was probably a stockholder in the St. Anthony Park Company when this street was named in 1885.

MARSHALL AVENUE: A man whose life was described as "swinging on the see-saw board of fate--a good many times up and a good many times down," William R. Marshall (1825-1896) was one of the developers of this street in 1855. Born in Missouri, he moved to Minnesota in 1849, and settled in St. Paul two years later as the first hardware merchant. Ten years after, he

founded the St. Paul Press, and was elected Governor of
Minnesota from 1866 to 1870. A tall, slender man with sandy
whiskers, small features, and a bald head, Marshall also
dabbled in real estate during much of his lifetime. There
is a county in Minnesota named for him.

MARYLAND AVENUE: Iglehart, Hall and Mackubin, natives of
Maryland, named this street in 1857.

MARY LANE: Platted in 1940 by John and Frances Moravec,
this street was named for their daughter.

MATILDA STREET: Remembered for her "bright, beautiful coun-
tenance with black hair and black eyes," Matilda (Whitall)
Rice (1827-1906) was the wife of Henry M. Rice for whom Rice
Street is named. Born in Rome, New York, she moved to
Richmond, Virginia, when she was seven. Matilda met Henry
Rice in Washington, D.C., where she was attending school,
and later married him in 1849.

MATTERHORN LANE: Leonard Bisanz, whose mother was born near
Berne, Switzerland, named this street in 1972. The plat is
the "Swiss Meadows Addition."

MAURY STREET: Matthew Fontaine Maury (1806-1873), a naval
officer and oceanographer, died the year this street was
named. Maury wrote several treatises on navigation, the
most important one a basic work on winds and currents of the
ocean which made possible a drastic reduction in sailing
times. A reserved, modest man, he had a world-wide reputation. Other streets named in this plat were for Stephen
Decatur (1752-1808), James Lawrence (1781-1813), Thomas
Truxtun (1755-1822), and Edward Preble (1761-1807), all
famous naval officers of the early nineteenth century.

MAY STREET: Named in 1881, this street name is most likely
a personal name; whose I cannot say.

MAYALL ALLEY: James H. Mayall, a real estate dealer, had a
residence on the alley when it was opened in 1879. His
brother, Samuel, was a prominent lawyer and real estate
dealer in the city for many years.

MAYNARD DRIVE: In 1951, Maynard Clough of Minnetonka Mills
was one of the six investors who purchased forty acres in
this area, and arranged for the construction of the Sibley
Manor apartments and the Sibley Plaza shopping center. The
developers were thought foolish to build an apartment complex
in what was then a sparsely settled area; however, the project was quite successful, and soon there was a waiting
list for the 550 apartment units.

MAYRE STREET: This street name, probably another form of
Mary, was platted in 1885 by Frederick and Robert Hager of
Atlanta, Georgia.

MAYWOOD STREET: Previously Coleman Street, the name was changed in 1940.

MECHANIC AVENUE: Mechanic has a general meaning of "skilled worker," an appropriate name for this street platted adjacent to the St. Paul Harvester Works, a large manufacturing plant which was located on the east side of Hazel Street.

MENDOTA STREET: Originally Oak Street, the name was changed by the City Council in 1872. The name Mendota is a Sioux word meaning mouth of a river.

MERCER STREET: At one time Clinton Street, the name was changed by the City Council in 1883. Mercer is a common place name, with a touch of elegance gained from the French "mer" meaning sea.

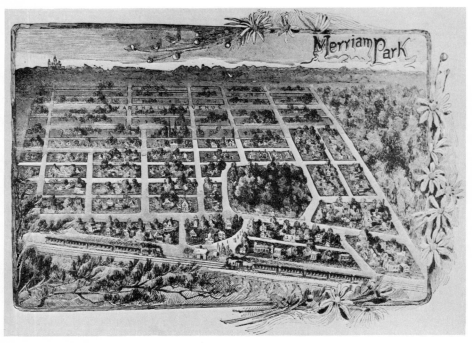

A "birds eye view" made in 1886 to promote the sale of lots.

MERRIAM LANE: Previously Terrace Park Avenue, the name was changed in 1940. John L. Merriam (1825-1895) and his son, William R. Merriam (1849-1931) were the developers of Merriam Park. John was one of the founders of the First National Bank, and a state legislator; William was active in politics, Governor of Minnesota from 1889-1893, and later director of the United States Census. Their residences

faced each other across Cedar Street above the Capitol
Building. One house was used for many years as the Science
Museum until torn down; the other house burned seventy years
ago, but the broad steps that led up to it remain at the end
of Sherburne Avenue.

MERRILL STREET: William C. Merrill, Jr. was sales manager
for Thomas Frankson, one of the developers of Chelsea Heights
in 1916. Merrill moved from St. Paul soon after.

MERRIMAC STREET: Named in 1889 as part of Riverside Park,
this is one of St. Paul's "ghost streets." Unmarked and
unimproved, the street is presently accessible only from
South St. Paul.

METCALF LANE: When the southern part of Hazel Avenue was
changed to Battle Creek Road in 1957, it became necessary
(to avoid confusion) to change Battle Creek Lane to Metcalf
Lane. The name comes from the addition platted in 1948 by
Allen A. and Elna Metcalf.

MICHAEL STREET: James C. Michael (1863-1946), a District
Court Judge in Ramsey County for thirty-one years, is
honored by this 1959 street name. Born in the state of
Virginia, he was raised on a farm and attended the country
schools. At twenty-one, he moved to Red Wing, where he
worked as a law office clerk, and was admitted to the Bar
in 1885. Four years later, he came to St. Paul where he
subsequently served as Corporation Counsel for the city.
In 1915, he was appointed a District Judge. An avid reader
and enthusiastic baseball fan, Michael was known for his
patience and tolerance.

MICHIGAN STREET: This street was named in 1851 for Lake
Michigan. Adjacent streets were named for Lakes Erie,
Ontario, Superior, and St. Clair.

MIDDLETON AVENUE: James Middleton (1833-1902) was reckoned
as one of the oldest and best informed real estate men in
the city at the time of his death. Born in Northern Ireland,
he came to Cottage Grove in Washington County about 1841.
He lived on the family farm there until 1881, when he moved
to St. Paul and entered the real estate business, naming
this street in 1887. Middleton was a state legislator in
1876, and was running for county commissioner the year of
his death.

MIDWAY PARKWAY: The Board of Park Commissioners for St. Paul
were quite concerned, in the 1890's, with some way to connect
the large parks together so they complemented one another.
Midway Parkway is a segment in the "trunk line of parkways"
they envisioned. Named in 1897, this parkway was to be a
link in the route beginning at Central Park, extending up
the hill past the State Capitol, north on Capitol Boulevard,

west on Como Avenue to Como Park, from Como Park to the State
Fairgrounds, through the Fairgrounds to St. Anthony Park,
from there in one direction to the University of Minnesota,
and in another direction to the Mississippi River Boulevard.
    Midway Parkway, a half-mile long connection between the
popular Como Park and State Fairgrounds, received its impetus
when the streetcar company installed their tracks and overhead
wires on Como Avenue, thus spoiling it as the approach to the
Park or Fairgrounds. As a result, the company paid the Park
Board $2,500 towards the grading of Midway Parkway, resulting
in its eventual completion.

MILFORD STREET: Originally platted as Spruce Street, the
name was changed in 1872. This name, if nondescript, does
have the advantage of being short and easy to pronounce.

MILLER CREST LANE: Carl S. and Agnes Miller platted this
street in 1954. The name is a compromise between the Millers
who wished the street called Miller Road, and the city
engineers who wished it called Crest Lane.

MILTON STREET: This street was named in 1871 for John Milton
(1608-1674) the English poet.

MINNEHAHA AVENUE: This street, a section line, was named in
1857 for Minnehaha Falls which had been immortalized two
years earlier in Longfellow's poem "Song of Hiawatha."
Minne means water, and haha means waterfall. Prior to 1849,
the falls were called Brown's Falls by the whites, and
Little Falls by the Indians.

MINNESOTA AVENUE: Originally termed Main Street, the Works
Progress Administration (WPA) officials felt there were
already too many "Main Streets," and this, the principal
thoroughfare within the State Fairgrounds, deserved a more
appropriate title.

MINNESOTA STREET: This is one of the original street names
of the city, applied in 1849. For over two centuries the
river we know as the Minnesota was called St. Peter's River,
a name bestowed by the early French explorers. When the
pioneers here were casting about for an Indian name to fit
the new territory--following the pattern of the other Midwest
states--they discovered the Indian name for the river. Soon
after a law was passed officially changing the name of the
river from the white man's name (St. Peter's) to the Indian
name (Minnesota).

MISSISSIPPI STREET: This important street in early St. Paul
was named in 1857 for the river. It was, for a time, the
main thoroughfare leading north from downtown, and served
then in somewhat the same way Interstate 35E does today.

MISSISSIPPI RIVER BOULEVARD: In 1887, Horace Cleveland,
Chicago landscape architect and consultant to the newly-
formed St. Paul Board of Park Commissioners, urged that the

A Sunday drive on the Mississippi River Boulevard just south of Marshall Avenue about 1910. The policeman on the bridge was stationed there to enforce the 8 MPH speed limit.

river shore between the two cities be preserved in their natural grandeur by laying out an avenue along the top of the bluffs on each side. Hindered first by the property owner's unreasonable prices, then by a depression and the building of a dam, the whole route was not finally acquired until 1907, the result of gifts, condemnation, purchase, and platting. It was opened two years later--with a watchman to keep away sharpshooting boys and their rifles. Another segment, planned from the High Bridge to the Fort Snelling bridge, was never built.

MISSOURI STREET: Originally Minnesota Street, the name was changed in 1883.

MITCHELL AVENUE: This street, named in 1959, is located on what was the eleven-acre farm of Simon Mitchell, an early pioneer in McLean Township, as it was then called. He was a clerk of the town board intermittently from 1859 to 1878. The name may also refer to William Mitchell (1874-1955), for many years a St. Paul lawyer, and Attorney General of the United States under President Hoover.

MOHAWK AVENUE: This is one of several Indian names applied in 1917 to the streets within Beaver Lake Heights.

MONROE COURT: Once Palace Place, the name was changed in 1942 to avoid confusion with Palace Avenue which is parallel, one block over. The name is that of the nearby high school.

MONTANA AVENUE: This street was named in 1886 for the state.

MONTCALM PLACE: Part of Lexington Park, this street was named in 1886 probably with reference to Marquis Louis Joseph de Montcalm De Saint-Veran (1712-1759). He was a French general killed when the British captured Quebec in 1759. The name was no doubt selected for its elegant sound, rather than any particular significance.

MONTGOMERY STREET: Originally Havana Street, the name was changed in 1886. The reason for this change, or who Montgomery might be is not recorded.

MONTREAL AVENUE: This street, on a one-half section line, was first surveyed as a county road in 1861. It was apparently graded and opened along at least part of its length in 1878, and it had its present name by 1892. However, it was not until the 1920's, with the development of Highland Park, that it assumed the dimensions of the main street it is today.

MONTROSE LANE: Introduced in the writings of Sir Walter Scott, a popular nineteenth century novelist, Montrose is a common name combining the elements of height and flowers. The name was applied here in 1887 by the Union Land Company.

MOORE STREET: James P. Moore was the land agent for Merriam Park, in charge of selling the lots, when this street was named in 1882. He worked closely with John L. Merriam and served for a time as his private secretary. Moore came to St. Paul about 1880, moved to Minneapolis in 1890, and left the area shortly thereafter.

MORGAN AVENUE: George H. Morgan, a clerk in the surveyor's office, may have been the source of this 1912 street name. He later ran a grocery store with his father on the East Side.

MORNINGSIDE DRIVE: See Berland Place.

MORTON STREET: This street was named in 1857, for whom I cannot say.

MOSES STREET: Originally named Chestnut Street, the name was changed in 1876. What significance the name has, if any, I do not know.

MOUND STREET: The Indian burial mounds, a few of which still remain in Mounds Park, prompted this street name in 1856. There were originally eighteen mounds in the area of the Park, and nineteen more along Dayton's Bluff. Today six remain.

MOUNDS BOULEVARD: Developed as part of Indian Mounds Park, the Boulevard was designed to connect with Phalen Park by way of Johnson Parkway. Mounds Boulevard was, at one time, projected in the other direction, winding across Swede Hollow, along the crest of Mt. Ida, down to Mississippi Street, up to Mt. Airy, and west to the State Capitol.

MT. AIRY STREET: This street was named in 1856 for the sense of airy, an adjective used quite frequently in the nineteenth century and an apt name for a high place. There is a suburb of Philadelphia entitled Mt. Airy because it is in a "high and airy position." The hill, I believe, took its name from the street.

The housing project presently occupying the hill was first planned in 1934 as an effort to clear it of small one and two-room shacks and squalid apartments that occupied the area at that time, and replace them with comfortable, low-cost housing. This plan, however, was not fulfilled until 1959 when 446 dwelling units were completed. If little else, this development does have one of the most spectacular views of the city.

MT. CURVE BOULEVARD: A common street name, bestowed here in 1915, by Den E. Lane.

MT. HOPE AVENUE: Applied here in 1874, this is a fairly common place name, including one use in Massachusetts, the native state of the developers.

MT. IDA STREET: It is written of John Warren, the developer of this street: "He had traveled extensively and acquired a varied knowledge; being a man of large means, he took the world quite easily, following the bent of his inclinations." Warren's education and travel are indicated by this 1853 street named for the mountain in central Crete where, according to Greek mythology, Zeus was hidden in a cave to save him from his father. While there, Zeus was tended by the nymphs Ida and Adrastea, and nurtured on goat milk and honey. It is a picturesque name for the area.

MULBERRY STREET: The mulberry tree provided this street name in 1862.

MUNSTER AVENUE: Possessing a statewide reputation, Andrew W. Munster (1853-1929) was a chief bridge engineer for St. Paul. Born in Norway, he immigrated to St. Paul in 1884 where he built several bridges, among them the High Bridge which is still standing. Although a favorite employee of the City Engineer, Munster later moved to Seattle.

MURPHY AVENUE: Franklin W. Murphy (1869-1940) was a Board Member of the Minnesota State Agricultural Society (which named this street within the State Fairgrounds) from 1910 to 1918, and President of that Society from 1919 to 1920.

Born in Wisconsin, he came to Minneapolis in 1891, and from
there he moved to Wheaton, Minnesota, in 1893. A lawyer by
profession, Murphy also owned a large farm near Wheaton
which was used as a demonstration station under the super-
vision of the State Agricultural School.

MURRAY STREET: Charles Murray (1868-195?) was the surveyor
of this street in 1924. He was born in Ireland and moved
to St. Paul in 1898 where he acted as a civil engineer and
surveyor, both for the county and in his own business, until
1947. This street was platted upon the Samuel and Elizabeth
Magoffin property.

MYRTLE AVENUE: Applied in 1881, this was a popular feminine
name at the time.

MYSTIC STREET: Mystic is a village in Connecticut, near
New London. Its name was borrowed by the Union Land Company
and applied here in 1888.

EDWARD DUFFIELD NEILL
clergyman, educator, historian
"a man of letters, a man of literature, a man of research, a man of thought"

NAGASAKI ROAD: It took the city three tries to get this name where they wanted it, but it was finally bestowed on the present street by the City Council in 1965. The name was a tribute to the city of Nagasaki, Japan, sister city of St. Paul, and Nagasaki's moral and economic virtues were extolled in the Council resolution initiating the name.

NASON PLACE: George L. Nason (1886-1949) was Superintendent of Parks in St. Paul from 1924 to 1932. Born in St. Paul, he graduated from the University of Minnesota engineering school, and subsequently took a postgraduate course at Harvard in architectural landscaping. From 1932 to 1936, he was Chief Inspector of Texas state parks, afterwards serving as district engineer for the National Park Service in Omaha. In later years, he served as consulting engineer and architect for the Capitol Approach project. Remembered as one of the finest Park Superintendents, he is honored by this 1967 street name within Como Park.

NEBRASKA AVENUE: This street was named in 1886 for the state.

NEIDERHOFFER STREET: Originally nameless, the City Council gave a name to this street in 1886. Jacob Neiderhoffer had a saloon in the immediate area, and later built a house on this street. He died at age sixty-five on November 21, 1891.

NEILL STREET: Almost a ghost street now, it was platted and named in 1852 for Edward D. Neill (1823-1893), clergyman, educator, and the first historian of Minnesota. Born in Philadelphia, he graduated from Amherst College and moved to St. Paul in 1849. He was subsequently a Presbyterian minister, State Superintendent of Public Instruction, Secretary to President Abraham Lincoln, Secretary of the Minnesota Historical Society, and President of Macalester College. Neill was considered independent, self-reliant, progressive, benevolent; a man of research and thought.

NELSON STREET: A soldier in the Confederate Army, Benjamin Franklin Nelson (1843-1928) came north to Minneapolis after the Civil War. From 1901 to 1907, he was Vice-President of

the Minnesota State Agricultural Society, the organization
responsible for the State Fair, and the naming of this
street within the Fairgrounds. During his term as President
of the Society from 1907 to 1909, Nelson remarked: "The
Fair may well be added to the list of the State's colleges,
and the visitor that will 'do' the Fair carefully, beginning with Division A, and going on leisurely and thought-
fully down the line to the end, will acquire a surprising
amount of valuable information--more than he could in the
same time in any other way."

NELSON STREET: Arthur E. Nelson (1892-1955) was Mayor of
St. Paul from 1922-1926. Born in Brown's Valley, Minnesota,
he graduated from Macalester College, attended law school,
and was admitted to the Bar in 1915. Five years later, he
was appointed Corporation Counsel for St. Paul where he
gained great popularity for his work in holding the streetcar company to their low rates. After his term as Mayor,
he ran for United States senator, but was defeated. This
street was named for him in 1959.

NETTLETON AVENUE: William Nettleton (1822-1905) was born
in Ohio, but moved to Minnesota in 1850 where he worked at
teaching farming to the Chippewa Indians near Crow Wing.
In 1853, he joined a land company which laid out the town
of Superior, Wisconsin. Three years later, in company with
his brother, he founded the city of Duluth. In 1871, he
purchased 130 acres near today's intersection of Randolph
Avenue and Lexington Parkway where he ran a dairy farm for
several years. He subdivided his farm here, platting this
street in 1886, and moved to Spokane, Washington where he
died.

NEVADA AVENUE: This street was named in 1886 for the state.

NEWCOME STREET: Charles B. Newcome was the President of
the St. Paul Harvester Works when this street was platted
in 1881. Their factory was close by.

NIAGARA STREET: Originally named Water Street, the name was
changed in 1883.

NILES AVENUE: Rudolph and Wilhelmina Knappheide, early
pioneers of the area who lived at Randolph and Cleveland
avenues named two streets in 1886: Niles and Detroit.
Both are cities in Michigan.

NINA STREET: Platted in 1854 by a group of developers, this
is most likely a personal name, but whose I cannot say.

NINTH STREET: In the early days of the city, a large reser-
voir was planned at the head of Ninth Street to catch the
abundant springs which flowed from the hillside there. It

was anticipated that such a waterworks could supply twenty feet of pressure at Jackson Street and Kellogg Boulevard. This street, the ninth from the river, was named in 1850.

NOKOMIS AVENUE: Used here as a street name in 1917, Nokomis is the grandmother of Hiawatha in The Song of Hiawatha (1855), a popular narrative poem by Longfellow. The word is actually the Chippewa term for "grandmother" used by Longfellow as a proper name.

NORBERT LANE: Norbert Bisanz was one of the brothers who developed this area in 1951. Both brothers have been in real estate most of their lives.

NORFOLK AVENUE: Previously part of Stewart Avenue, this section of the street was renamed in 1940. Norfolk is a common English name.

NORPAC ROAD: The Northern Pacific (now Burlington Northern) railroad tracks which parallel the street prompted this name in 1965.

NORTH STREET: This street was the north border of the plat filed in 1852.

NORTH PARK DRIVE: This street was named by the city in 1961 because it follows the north side of Battle Creek Park.

NORTON STREET: Opened in 1925, this street is probably a namesake of either John or Edward Norton, real estate men.

NORTONIA STREET: This name, applied in 1917, is attributed as a compliment to John W. and William W. Norton, real estate dealers of St. Paul. William left for San Diego in 1918; John (1872-1956) remained in St. Paul to become one of the most prominent and long-lived real estate dealers.

NUGENT STREET: This 1882 name is possibly that of John Nugent, an employee of the nearby railroad.

NUSBAUMER DRIVE: Frederick Nusbaumer (1850-1935) was called the "father of the St. Paul park system" for his work as Superintendent of Parks from 1889 to 1922. Born in Baden, Germany, he attended the Polytechnical School in Freiburg. Upon graduation at seventeen, he went to London where he worked in the famous Kew Gardens, after which he traveled to France where he worked in its largest nursery. In France, he met Horace W. H. S. Cleveland, then recognized as one of the world's leading landscape architects, who urged him to come to the United States. Nusbaumer immigrated to St. Paul in 1878 and did contract landscaping for twelve years until becoming Superintendent. His skill made Como Park nationally famous as a garden spot. This street within the Park was named in his honor in 1967.

OAKDALE AVENUE: Applied here in 1874, this is a very common place name.

OAKGROVE PLACE: John and Helen Merriam named this street in 1886.

OAK VIEW COURT: This street was named in 1965 because it overlooked a clump of oaks.

OAKLAND AVENUE: This very common name was applied here in 1871.

OAKLEY AVENUE: Given in 1884, this street name, like the others in Union Park, was almost surely chosen for its pleasing and somewhat exotic sound. Oakley contains the sound of oak, a tree noted for its strength and permanence.

OAKRIDGE STREET: Part of Burlington Heights, this street was named in 1888.

OCEAN STREET: Most likely prompted by the adjacent street, Atlantic, this street name was given in 1882 by Charles Leonard, a contractor.

OGDEN AVENUE: Previously Chester Avenue, the name was changed in 1940.

OHIO STREET: Once Randall Street, the name was changed in 1880. Like other streets in the area, it was named for the state.

OLD HUDSON ROAD: When Hastings Avenue was changed to Hudson Road in 1940, the previous Hudson Road became Old Hudson Road.

OLIVE STREET: There were, at different times, several Olive streets within the city. This one was named in 1852 for the tree.

DAVID OLMSTED
The first Mayor of St. Paul

OLMSTEAD STREET: Characterized as: "A well-built man; pleasant in his address; quiet in his manners; sensible in his speech; naturally polite, and a real gentleman," David Olmsted (1822-1861) was the first Mayor of St. Paul in 1854-55. Among other occupations, Olmsted was a miner, farmer, Indian trader, legislator, and newspaper editor. Olmsted County is said to be named for him. It is perhaps symbolic that even the most diligent would be hard pressed to find this opened, but unmarked street which originally was called Spring Street, but was renamed (and misspelled) in 1872.

OLYMPIA AVENUE: Previously Temple Street, the name was changed in 1940.

OMABAN STREET: Named in 1892, this is one of the most perplexing of all the street names, and I cannot even conjecture as to what it might signify. I suspect it is a coined word.

OMAHA STREET: Originally platted as Ontario Street, the name was changed in 1872. The name undoubtedly indicates Omaha, Nebraska, the ultimate destination of the railroad whose tracks and shops are adjacent to the street.

ONEGA STREET: Originally Mendota Street, the name was changed in 1876. Onega appears to be an Indian word of uncertain meaning.

ONEIDA STREET: Oneida is a small village in Madison County, New York, famous for its communist experiment and the silverware that bears its name. That village is named for the Oneida tribe, one of the six tribes of the Iroquois League. This street was named in 1856.

ORANGE AVENUE: Iglehart, Hall and Mackubin, natives of Maryland, may have had that more temperate climate in mind when naming this street in 1857.

Located where Como Avenue and Victoria Avenue would cross, this is Henry McKenty's house on Lake Como (about 1855). The little girl in front may be his daughter, Josephine, for whom the lake is named.

ORCHARD AVENUE: Previously Locust Street, the name was changed in 1874. The property in this area around Como Lake was first developed by Henry McKenty (1821-1869) who moved to St. Paul in 1851. A bustling little man, McKenty named Como Lake (which had previously been known as Sandy Lake or McKenty's Lake) as well as Lake Josephine (for his daughter) and Lake Johanna (for his wife). McKenty lost his money and property in the depression of 1857 and later ended his life. Both his wife and daughter also committed suicide.

ORLEANS STREET: This street was named by the City Council
in 1883.

ORME COURT: James E. Orme (1865-1941) for whom this street
was named in 1927, married a daughter of the Bohland family,
pioneer farmers of the area. He was a prominent Mason, and
treasurer of the Washington foundry in St. Paul.

ORRIN STREET: Orrin Curtis, an insurance agent, took a
lease on the Cullen house, (which remains at 698 Stewart
Avenue), in 1866, and was apparently remembered when this
street was named in 1874.

OSAGE STREET: Originally Oak Street, the name was changed
in 1874. The Osage are a tribe of North American plains
Indians found in Missouri, Kansas, and Oklahoma.

OSCEOLA AVENUE: Osceola (1800?-1838) was a famous Seminole
warrior who fought against the white man in the Florida
Everglades. Despite that fact, he was a popular and romantic
figure when this street was named in 1871. This is one of
very few St. Paul streets that run north, south, east, and
west.

OTIS AVENUE: Part of Desnoyer Park, this street was named
in 1887 by Frank Newell, a civil engineer with the firm
Hawley and Newell. Mary C. Otis, his wife, was the daughter
of George L. Otis, Mayor of St. Paul in the 1860's.

OTSEGO STREET: This street was named in 1853 for a county
and lake in New York state made famous by James Fenimore
Cooper's "Leatherstocking" novels. Otsego Hall in Coopers-
town was also the name of Cooper's boyhood home, for a long
time the most notable private residence in that part of
New York state.

OTTAWA AVENUE: Applied here in 1855, this was one of a
series of Indian names, in this case, that of the Ottawa
tribe who occupied much of Michigan.

OTTO AVENUE: Leberich (1812-1884) and Carolina Otto came
here from Prussia around 1860. They purchased a forty-acre
farm in what is today the area between Cleveland and Prior
avenues, Highland Parkway and Bohland Avenue, including the
area now occupied by the Highland Shopping Center. The
street was first named in 1881, but in 1934 the western
part was renamed Highland Parkway because it ran between
Highland Park and the Mississippi River Boulevard. Otto was
a skilled musician and band leader who played at many early
dances and celebrations in the city.

OXFORD STREET: Platted as Linden Street in 1871, the name
was changed a year later. This is an English name chosen
to fit with the others in the area.

P

PACIFIC STREET: Originally Central and Centennial avenues, the name was changed in 1883. This name was simply transferred from another street within the city.

PACKARD STREET: Probably referring to some investor, this street was named in 1885 as part of St. Anthony Park.

PAGE STREET: This street was named in 1857 as part of the West Side; for whom I cannot say.

PALACE AVENUE: While there were many Cottage streets, there was only one Palace Avenue. This name was chosen in 1854, most likely for its appeal to the future home builder.

PALMER PLACE: Edward G. Rogers and his wife, Mary platted this street in 1883. Palmer is probably a personal name-- one guess might be Edward Palmer, a fellow lawyer, and general counsel for the railroad nearby.

PARK STREET: The word conveys an idea of natural unspoiled beauty which made it an appealing street name in 1854.

PARKLAND COURT: This name was applied in 1970 because, as the developer explained, it just sounded nice.

PARKVIEW AVENUE: Named in 1928, the street leads to a view overlooking Como Park.

PARKWAY DRIVE: Originally a county road (which accounts for its diagonal course), and later called White Bear Road, the name was changed to Parkway Drive in 1927. This name refers, I assume, to nearby Wheelock Parkway.

PARNELL STREET: Previously without a name, the street was so designated in 1886. The name may have been selected as a reference to Charles S. Parnell (1846-1891), Irish political leader. Supported by the Irish in the United States, Parnell was the force seeking and winning Home Rule for Ireland.

PARTRIDGE ROAD: Donald H. Partridge was President of his construction company when he developed this street in 1972.

PASCAL STREET: Blaise Pascal (1623-1662) was a French geometrician, philosopher, and writer. A man of incredible brilliance, Pascal was, as a child, such a zealous student that books were denied to him for a while; nonetheless, he re-invented geometry at the age of twelve. After making many contributions to mathematics and physics, he renounced the world at age thirty-one, and joined a monastery where he wrote on theology and philosophy. The street was named in 1881 because of its proximity to Hamline University.

PAYNE AVENUE: Rice W. Payne (1818-1884) was a Virginia gentleman from Warrenton. Member of an influential family and a successful lawyer in his own right, Payne visited St. Paul in 1856 that he might see and experience what was then the Far West. While here, he invested $1000 in some lots on the East Side, returning soon after to Virginia, where he subsequently served as a Major in the Confederate Army. According to family tradition (which is questionable), Payne's lots in St. Paul were confiscated after the Civil War on the grounds that Payne was a rebel, but it was not until after his death that a suit was brought to recover damages for the confiscated property.

PEARL STREET: Opened as Pym Street, the name was changed in 1910.

PEDERSEN STREET: Jens Pedersen (1866-1941) was a civil engineer who worked for the city for many years before going into business on his own. Born in Norway, he immigrated to St. Paul with his parents after the Civil War. A hard-working, dedicated man, the city engineer's office had a party to honor him in 1917 when they named the street.

Looking south on Payne Avenue from York Avenue about 1935. Almost every building pictured is still standing.

PELHAM BOULEVARD: This Boulevard was named in 1887, like
many other street names in the area, for a resort village
near New York City, in Westchester County, bordering on
Long Island Sound. At that time, the village contained a
number of elegant country houses, an association which
made it a desirable street name.

PENNOCK AVENUE: A man of considerable literary and musical
ability, Pennock Pusey (1825-1903) was a real estate dealer
and friend of the Tatum family who platted this addition in
1885. He moved to St. Paul in 1854, served as Assistant
Secretary of State, and was later private secretary to
Governor Pillsbury. In 1888, he returned to his family
home at Wilmington, Delaware. Another street, now named
Howell, was then called Pusey.

PENNSYLVANIA AVENUE: This street was named in 1856 for
the state.

PETIT STREET: Petit means small, an appropriate name for
this twenty-foot alley.

PHALEN DRIVE: This was named as one of the streets within
Phalen Park by the City Council in 1967. The name, of
course, is derived from the lake, which is named for Edward
Phalen (or Felyn) born in Londonderry, Ireland, about 1811.
He immigrated to New York City where he enlisted in the army
in 1835, and was subsequently assigned to Fort Snelling. He
was discharged from the army at the end of his three-year
term whereupon he made a claim in what is now downtown St.
Paul. Six feet, two-and-a-half inches tall, with brown hair
and gray eyes, he was a commanding figure, but unfortunately
his personality was not. He boasted of the lawless and
criminal life he had led before the army, and neighbors here
reported him immoral, cruel, revengeful, and unscrupulous.
Phalen soon sold this first claim and took another in the
area today bounded by Case, Edgerton, Minnehaha avenues and
the railroad tracks. A creek flowing near this claim took
its owner's name, and became Phalen's Creek, and by extension, the lake drained by this creek became known as
Phalen's Lake, even though he did not live near its shores.
This second claim was sold in 1844 for seventy dollars to
William Dugas. Phalen was later tried for the murder of
his partner, acquitted and re-indicted, whereupon he fled
toward California. It was reported that he was killed, in
self-defense, by his traveling companions in that same
year, 1850.

PIEDMONT STREET: Applied in 1888, this was a popular name
of the eighteenth century, meaning literally, foot of the
mountain. By suggesting height, and with a foreign sound
to it, it was an appealing name which, rather than any
local significance, would account for its choice.

PIERCE STREET: Franklin Pierce (1804-1869) was United States President at the time this street was named in 1856. There was once a Pierce County in Minnesota, but Pierce's respect for state's rights, and his opposition to Lincoln made him unpopular after the Civil War, and the county name was changed.

PIERCE BUTLER ROUTE: Previously the Northern Route, the name was changed by the City Council in 1961 to honor Pierce Butler, Jr. (1893-1957), lawyer and civic leader. Born in St. Paul, the son of Pierce Butler, a United States Supreme Court Justice, he graduated from Princeton University in 1914, and Harvard Law School in 1917. Returning to St. Paul, he associated with a local law firm where his quick wit and turn of phrase earned him the respect of judges. Outside his law practice, he was active in the United World Federalists, St. Paul United Improvement Council, and many other organizations. During the last years of his life, he also served as Mexican consul in St. Paul.

PIGSEYE LAKE ROAD: This road was sold to the city in 1926 by the Chicago, Milwaukee, St. Paul Railroad. The lake takes its name from the notorious "Pigs Eye" Parrant who, along with his fellow French-Canadian voyageurs, lived for a time in this area during the earliest days of the city.

PILLSBURY STREET: Originally Main Street, the name was changed in 1886. This new name may refer to Charles F. Pillsbury (1828-1888), a lawyer engaged in the real estate business. Born in Maine, he moved to Minneapolis in 1854 and was subsequently in business with Allan and Eustis, real estate dealers in this area.

PINE STREET: It is written that in 1851 when this street was named, there was a steam sawmill at the foot of Olive Street, and the pine logs sawed there suggested this name.

PINEHURST AVENUE: Hurst is an Anglo-Saxon word revived in the nineteenth century meaning wooded hill, and it is often coupled with tree names, as in this case, and the case of Oakhurst, Lynnhurst, and the like. The name, applied here in 1919, has no particular significance, other than a fashionable sound.

PINE VIEW COURT: The street overlooked a clump of pines when it was named in 1965.

PLATO AVENUE: Originally called Flint Street and Fay Street, the name was changed in 1883. Plato was a popular name for railroad stations of the day because it was short and easy to spell. The same advantages apply to its use as a street name.

PLEASANT AVENUE: This street was named in 1851, most likely for the favorable connotation of the word. There are over a thousand places with this same name in our country.

PLUM STREET: This street was named in 1857 for the fruit.
The adjacent street is called Cherry.

POINT DOUGLAS ROAD: Point Douglas was an important community in early Minnesota history because it marked the con-
fluence of the St. Croix and Mississippi rivers, and there
were several roads by this name. The first road followed
along the river bank to Red Rock, while the present road
took the higher ground, a course later followed closely by
Highway #61.

POND STREET: I cannot find any evidence of a pond in the
vicinity when this street was named in 1888.

PORTLAND AVENUE: With its somewhat stately tone, this was
a popular name of the nineteenth century which ultimately
derives from the Isle of Portland in England which has a
sixteenth century castle, and other romantic associations.
This street was named in 1871.

POWERS AVENUE: Winn Powers (1861-1939) was Mayor of St. Paul
from 1914-1916, and a long-time Democratic state leader.
Born and educated in Ohio, he moved to St. Paul in 1884 where
he established the Odd Fellows Review, one of the most influential fraternal publications in the country. Powers
remained editor and publisher of the magazine throughout his
life, while serving five terms as Councilman, and later,
Mayor. This street was named in 1959 by the City Council.

PREBLE STREET: Edward Preble (1761-1807) was an American
naval officer well remembered when this street was named in
1873. At the age of sixteen, Preble ran away to sea, was
active in the Revolutionary War and subsequently worked in
the merchant service. He was a Commander in the Barbary
Wars, and in charge of the assault on Tripoli.

PRESCOTT STREET: This street was named in 1874, most likely
for Charles A. Prescott, an early settler in the area who
owned a farm above Wabasha Street on what is today Prospect
Terrace, but was then called Prescott's Point. He, with
his sons and wife, ran a pawnbroker's shop in the city.

PRINCE STREET: Originally Third Street, the name was changed
in 1872. "A good and very popular public officer," John S.
Prince (1821-1895) was five times Mayor of St. Paul in the
1860's. Born in Cincinnati, he came to St. Paul in 1854 as
the agent of a fur trading company. While here, he super-
intended an early sawmill near the street now bearing his
name. Prince held a number of offices, both public and
private, and was accounted one of the leading citizens of
the day.

PRINCETON AVENUE: This was named in 1883, like the other
streets within Macalester Park, for a college, in this case
Princeton University in New Jersey.

PRIOR AVENUE: Charles Henry Prior (1833-1921) was born in Connecticut and moved to Ohio in 1837. He was educated in Cleveland, and traveled to Minnesota with the railroads in 1858. A civil engineer by profession, he held many posts with several railroad companies before joining the Chicago, Milwaukee and St. Paul Railroad. In 1879, while laying out the track between Minneapolis and St. Paul (Short Line), he, with John L. Merriam, bought and platted Merriam Park alongside the tracks, naming this street in 1882. Besides his activity in railroad construction, he was a founder of the streetcar, electric light, and telephone companies of Minneapolis. Prior Lake in Scott County is also named for him.

PRISCILLA STREET: Priscilla Mullens was the wife of John Alden. Their names are immortalized in The Courtship of Miles Standish by Longfellow, a popular poem when this street was named in 1885.

PROSPECT TERRACE: This street was named in 1855 for its position on top of the bluff where it provides quite a prospect, or view.

PROSPERITY AVENUE: This street was named in 1884 for the dictionary definition of success, good fortune, etc. A bisecting street (now Barclay) was named Amity, meaning peace and friendship. By checking the city map, you can find the road to Prosperity.

QUIRNIA AVENUE: This street was named in 1927 as part of the estate of Peter Bohland, a pioneer farmer of the area. Both Quirnia and Xina (now Hampshire Avenue) were applied at this time; both seem to have been chosen for their exotic connotations.

*Looking towards downtown on West Seventh Street from Ramsey Street about
1917.   Fire Station No. 1 has replaced the Liberty Bond billboard.*

R

RACE STREET: This 1881 street name most likely indicates a personal name.

RALEIGH STREET: Sir Walter Raleigh (1552?-1618), an English military and naval commander who made several early explorations of North America, was a popular figure when this street was named in 1885.

RAMLOW PLACE: William G. Ramlow (1885-   ) was a civil and mining engineer, as well as a registered land surveyor when this street was platted in 1946. After a stint in the United States Army Corps of Engineers during World War II, he started his own engineering firm and worked with Kenneth Bordner in platting this addition. Audrey Street in West St. Paul is named for his daughter.

RAMSEY STREET: Alexander Ramsey (1815-1903) was territorial governor of Minnesota when this street was named in 1849. Much has been written about Ramsey's many successes; perhaps the secret lies in one description of him: "He is exceedingly cordial in his ways; makes everybody think he is a personal friend; avoids any remark which might give offense, and in case of a sudden rumpus you will always find him missing. When he does get into trouble, however, he is like a steamboat, backs out gracefully."

RANDALL AVENUE: Secretary of the Minnesota State Agricultural Society from 1895 to 1907, during the period of its
greatest development, Eugene Wilson Randall (1859-1940) was
also at various times a farmer, an editor, and Dean of the
University of Minnesota Department of Agriculture. Honored
by this street name within the Fairgrounds, Randall was
born in Winona, but later lived in Morris and St. Paul. At
the beginning of Randall's administration, bicycle tricks
and races were all the rage; at the end of his administration, automobile performances were among the most popular
events.

RANDALL STREET: Considered "the biggest man in town" when
this street was named in 1853, William H. Randall (1806-1861)
was born in Massachusetts, but moved to St. Paul in 1846
with considerable money which he invested in real estate.
Although the property he owned was later worth millions of
dollars, the severe depression of 1857, and Randall's death
a short time later prevented him from realizing any profit
on his investments.

RANDOLPH AVENUE: This street was said to be named, in 1857,
for the famous Virginia family descended from William
Randolph (1651-1711). Members of this family served in the
Continental Congress and early United States Congresses, as
well as holding other important posts in the Federal and
state governments. Thomas Jefferson, for whom Jefferson
Avenue was named, was related by marriage to the Randolph
family.

RANKIN STREET: Rhodes B. and Lizzie K. Rankin of Louisville,
Kentucky, owned extensive property around lower Randolph
Avenue when this street was named in 1872.

RASH AVENUE: Originally Railroad Avenue, the name was
changed in 1886. I cannot help but wonder if someone in
the city engineer's office said: "Let's not do anything
rash," and his office mate replied: "That's a fine name."
Less fanciful, but more probable is that the street is a
personal surname.

RAVOUX STREET: Augustin Ravoux (1815-1906) was a Roman
Catholic priest when this street was named in 1871. Born
in France, he traveled to this country in 1836, was ordained
in 1840, and embarked on missionary work among the Sioux
Indians the following year. From the departure of Father
Galtier in 1844, until the arrival of Bishop Cretin in 1851,
Father Ravoux was in charge of the entire Catholic Church in
this area. In his later years, Father Ravoux was arranging
some drapery in the church and had his mouth full of pins.
He fell and some of the pins passed into his windpipe and
stuck in his throat. Needless to say, this affected his
preaching.
    This street name was discontinued for a short time, but

at the urging of the Ravoux grand assembly of the Knights of Columbus, the name was restored.

RAYMOND AVENUE: Bradford P. Raymond (1846-1916) was a college president when this street was named in 1885. Born in Connecticut, he was a student at Hamline University after the Civil War. He was elected President of Lawrence University, Appleton, Wisconsin, from 1883-1889 and was later President of Wesleyan University in Middletown, Connecticut.

REANEY AVENUE: Master of many steamboats, Captain John H. Reaney (1836-1882) was born in Pittsburgh, moved to St. Paul with his father in 1852, and at an early age, began steamboating with Louis Robert. Remembered as a very kind and congenial man, Reaney was honored by this street named for him in 1872.

RED ROCK ROAD: The city accepted this street within the Red Rock Industrial District from the Port Authority in 1969. Both the District and the street take their name from the Red Rock, a large granite stone which was located on the bank of the Mississippi River at what is now Newport. This boulder, a sacred shrine of the Sioux Indians, is now on the grounds of the Newport Methodist Church.

RESERVE STREET: Platted as Minnesota Street, the present name comes from proximity to what was, in the 1850's, a large tract of land known as McLean's Reservation. Lying between Mound, Burns, Griffith streets and Highway 12, this sixty-three acre tract, the property of Nathaniel McLean, had a lake in the center.

RETURN COURT: Opened in 1946 on an easement from the adjacent railroad, this street apparently takes its name from the circle route which it completes.

RICE STREET: Tall and slender, with a fine head upon his shoulders, and a commanding presence, Henry M. Rice (1816-1894) was a delegate from Minnesota Territory to the United States Senate when this street was named in 1857. Born in Vermont, Rice journeyed to Fort Snelling in 1839 where he engaged in the fur trade and negotiated several Indian treaties. A decade later, with his family, he paddled a birch-bark canoe from Mendota down the Mississippi River to St. Paul where he later built the first residence on Summit Avenue. Here he traded heavily in real estate, gave Rice Park to the city, and vigorously promoted both St. Paul and Minnesota. Rice, along with Alexander Ramsey and Henry Sibley, were probably the most influential of the early pioneers.

RICHMOND STREET: Thomas Daly, a well-to-do young man from Canada named three streets in 1856: Canada (since changed to Colborne Street), Duke, and Richmond. The obvious inference would be that they honored the Fourth Duke of Richmond, Governor General of Canada in 1818-1819.

RIDGE STREET: This name was chosen in 1881 to reflect the street's position on the hill.

RIVERVIEW AVENUE: Although it may not have been true when this street was named in 1874, the West Side area as early as 1900, has been known as Riverview, a less geographically confusing name. Originally designated as the west side of the Mississippi River, the residents of the area, in 1917, officially adopted Riverview as their new name, and the telephone exchange and post office were renamed accordingly. However, the new name has not persisted and most today refer to it again as the West Side.

RIVERWOOD PLACE: Originally part of Ashland Avenue, the name was changed in 1922 as part of a general renaming in the area.

RIVOLI STREET: Rivoli is a town in Italy at the foot of
the Alps in the province of Torino. An old castle distinguished this nineteenth century tourist village when this
street was named in 1853. The developer, John E. Warren,
was a literary man and inveterate world traveler.

ROBBINS STREET: Daniel M. Robbins (1830-1905) was a
leading businessman in St. Paul when this street was named
in 1885. He had large investments in real estate and was
very active in the organization of the Minnesota Transfer
Company, near the street bearing his name. Robbins was
also president of the Northwestern Elevator Company which
owned more than a hundred elevators along the Great
Northern Railway tracks.

ROBERT STREET: A tall, muscular man of great energy, with
strong features and decided convictions, Captain Louis
Robert (1811-1874) was a fur trader on the Missouri River
before moving to St. Paul in 1844, where he purchased part
of the original townsite, and named this street in 1849.
The owner of several steamboats which he piloted, Robert
also dealt heavily in real estate ending life with considerable money and a reputation for generosity and public
spirit. Since Robert was French-Canadian, his name was
originally pronounced "Row-bear."

ROBIE STREET: Originally named Oak Street, the name was
changed in 1876. Robie is undoubtedly a personal surname,
but whose I cannot say.

ROBLYN AVENUE: Formerly part of Rondo Avenue (since obliterated by Interstate 94), the name was changed to Roblyn in
1913. This street name, and the Roblyn Park Addition in
which it appears are a combination of the names Orlando A.
Robertson and Frederick B. Lynch (1866-1934), developers of
the subdivision. Robertson was President of the U.S. Farm
Lands Company; he moved to Sacramento, California, in 1913.
Lynch, born in Madison, Wisconsin, graduated from college
at Yankton, South Dakota, and moved to St. Paul in 1897
where he was president of the Southern Colonization Company.
Lynch was active in Democratic politics and was once men-
tioned as a candidate for a cabinet post under President
Wilson in 1912. In 1918 he moved to New York, and later to
Orlando, Florida, where he died.

ROCKWOOD AVENUE: George E. Rockwood platted this street in
1884. He came to St. Paul about 1874 and was associated
with the St. Paul branch of a Chicago clothing firm. He
left the city about 1886.

ROGERS STREET: Edward G. Rogers (1842-1910) was a lawyer
and a representative in the state legislature when this
street was named in 1887. Born in Michigan, he graduated
from law school there, and moved to St. Paul in the early

1870's where he became prominent in Republican politics. At the time of his death, he was a member of the City Council.

ROME AVENUE: Rome A. Schaffner was President of the Highland Park Company when this street was platted in 1925. A resident of St. Paul from 1906 to 1930, he apparently left the city at that time. For most of his residence here, he was chief clerk for a construction company.

The paving of Rome Avenue in 1927. The Highland Water Tower is under construction in the background. The houses at the left are all on Hillcrest Avenue; numbers 1726, 1720, 1701, 1706, 1700, 1665, 1690, 1661, 1672, 1660.

ROSE AVENUE: This street was named in 1857 for the flower by the developers, Iglehart, Hall and Mackubin.

ROSEN ROAD: Milton Rosen (1893-1970) was a member of the St. Paul City Council for thirty years, most of which time he held the post of Public Works Commissioner. Born in the slums of Chicago, Rosen moved to St. Paul as a child. In 1915 he established the Milton Rosen Tire Company which he managed until 1962. Opinionated, sometimes cantankerous, Rosen engaged in countless civic, charitable, and public service activities during his long residence in St. Paul. This street was named in 1957.

<u>ROSS AVENUE</u>: William H. Ross was in business with John Weide, a brother of one of the developers of this street in 1872. Ross may have invested in the property.

<u>ROWE PLACE</u>: This street was platted in 1953 by Herbert J. Rowe, of the firm Rowe and Knudson, which dealt in real estate and insurance.

<u>ROY STREET</u>: Frank and Charlotte Holstrom named this street in 1909, most likely for Roy Holstrom, a surveyor.

<u>RUSSELL STREET</u>: This street was laid out about 1890 on land adjacent to Phalen Creek. The identity of Russell is neither recalled nor recorded.

<u>RUTH STREET</u>: Ruth was the daughter of Angier and Luella B. Ames, the developers of this street in 1890. Ruth taught briefly at the Harrison School where her mother was Principal. At the time of her mother's death in 1915, she was the wife of Waldo F. Kelly of Providence, Rhode Island.

<u>RYAN AVENUE</u>: Previously Franklin Street, the name was changed in 1940 to avoid duplication. Harry, Richard, and Emmett Ryan were officers of the St. Paul Milk Company located on this street.

<u>RYDE STREET</u>: Ryde is a city in Lancaster County, England. The street was named in 1885 when English names were in vogue.

S

ST. ALBANS STREET: Platted as Prairie Street in 1871, the name was changed the following year. St. Albans is the site of one of the oldest Roman towns in England.

ST. ANTHONY AVENUE: This name has been applied to several streets within the city at various times, most notably that portion of Kellogg Boulevard running from St. Peter Street up to the Cathedral. This early street, and the continuations westward, took their name from the fact they were part of an early road between St. Paul and St. Anthony (now southeast Minneapolis). The Cathedral hill was for many years known as St. Anthony Hill for the fact it was accessible by this street. The present street of this name, the north frontage road of Interstate Highway 94, was designated in 1964.

ST. CLAIR AVENUE: This street was named in 1851 for Lake St. Clair, between Lakes Huron and Erie. Adjacent streets were Michigan, Superior, Ontario, Erie, and Huron. St. Clair, west of Dale Street, follows the course of the first east-west road in that area, a Reserve Township road laid out in December, 1858.

ST. LAWRENCE STREET: Originally Kittering Street (for Jefferson F. Kittering who platted the addition in 1857), the name was changed in 1883. St. Lawrence is a common name and most local usage refers to the river, one of the largest in North America.

ST. PAUL AVENUE: Over the years, there have been many St. Paul Avenues. This latest was named in 1924.

ST. PETER STREET: This is one of the original streets of the city, named in 1849 for the St. Peter or Minnesota River. The river was first mentioned as St. Peter's River in 1689, and it was known to the French and English explorers by that name for more than 150 years. In 1852, the name was officially changed to the Minnesota River, which was the Indian name.

SALEM STREET: This is one address for those who don't like
people dropping in on them. One of St. Paul's "ghost
streets," the only present access is to launch a boat from
South St. Paul and paddle across the Mississippi. Named in
1889 as part of Riverside Park, the street could acknowledge
any one of several cities, the oldest and best known being
Salem, Massachusetts.

SANDRALEE DRIVE: Sandralee is the daughter of Ralph and
Emily Peterson who platted their twenty-nine acre hobby farm
in 1960. An adjacent street was already named Darlene, the
name of one Peterson daughter; this coincidence suggested
the name of the second daughter.

SARATOGA STREET: This street was named in 1874 by John Wann,
an Englishman, at the instigation of his wife, an American.
She felt some redress was needed for the many British names
(Avon, Oxford, Milton) so she suggested this name in honor
of the battle of Saratoga--the turning point of the Revolutionary War--in which the Americans soundly defeated the
British.

SARGENT AVENUE: Edwin and Electa Sargent were the developers
of this street named in 1883. He was born in Vermont about
1823, and moved to St. Paul about 1883 where he engaged in
the real estate business. His wife was born in New York
about 1826. They both moved to Redlands, California, in
1895.

SAUNDERS AVENUE: The Saunders family owned an eighty-acre
estate bounded by Bohland, Montreal, Fairview, and Cleveland
avenues. Edward N. Saunders (1845-1913) came to St. Paul
in 1870 where he soon conceived the idea of shipping coal to
Minnesota through the Great Lakes. With James J. Hill, he
founded the Northwestern Fuel Company which proved highly
profitable. Edward N. Saunders, Jr. (1877-1953) graduated
from Yale with a Ph.D. in 1899, then returned to St. Paul
where he later took control of the family business, one of
the largest in the North Central area. This street was
named in 1924 when their estate was subdivided into building
lots.

SCENIC PLACE: Previously Suburban Place, the name was
changed in 1957 to avoid confusion with Suburban Avenue, one
block adjacent.

SCHEFFER AVENUE: Originally Snelling Street, the name was
changed in 1886. Albert Scheffer (1844-1905) was born in
Germany but immigrated to St. Paul in 1859 and soon after
became a teller in a Stillwater bank owned by his brother.
After fighting in the Civil War, he went into the banking
business, with which he remained for most of his life. He
also served in the state senate and was an active member of
the school board. He was interested in civic affairs, well
regarded by most, and his son-in-law, William Hamm, was a
member of the City Council.

SCHERERS LANE: This street is part of an addition made by A. J. Scherer about 1888. He apparently never lived in St. Paul.

SCHEUNEMAN AVENUE: This street was platted in 1883 by Anna Ramsey, but it was not named at that time.

SCHLETTI STREET: This street was platted in 1916 by Elizabeth, the widow of Christian Schletty. The Schletty family moved to St. Paul from Red Wing in the 1870's, and over the years acquired a good deal of property northwest of Maryland and Western avenues. Overlooking their property, high on the bluff, they built the family home, which still stands at 503 Orange Street. Another Schletty home remains at 1275 Mackubin Street. Christian's son Fred was a veteran nurseryman and State Fair official. The change of the last letter from "y" to "i" was apparently a whim of Elizabeth.

SCHROEDER DRIVE: The St. Paul City Council named this street in 1956 for Alfred H. Schroeder (1901-1974), City Architect at the time. Graduating from St. Thomas College in 1921 with a degree in civil engineering, he worked for private firms until becoming an assistant engineer for the city in 1935. When he returned to St. Paul after World War II, he was hired to modernize the city building code.

SCOTT ROAD: This street is said to be named in 1958 for Scott, son of Grege Beckett, Plat Commissioner at the time and/or Scott, the grandson of Hyman J. Goldberg, office engineer in the Department of Public Works.

SCUDDER STREET: Reverend John L. Scudder was pastor of the First Congregational Church of Minneapolis when this street was named in 1885. He most likely had a financial interest in the property.

SEAL STREET: One of several streets named in 1887 as part of St. Anthony Park South, this probably was inspired by a personal name.

SEAMER STREET: Leonard C. Seamer (1888-1959) was city valuation engineer at the time the city named this street in 1956. Born in Cincinnati, he came to St. Paul as a youth, and began his career with the city in 1911 as a clerk in the Department of Public Works. He subsequently served as assistant land commissioner, chairman of the city technical committee, and since 1928, assessment and valuation engineer. He was also responsible for bringing the National Majorette championship to St. Paul in 1941, where it has been held ever since as part of the Winter Carnival.

SEARLE STREET: Olaf and Dagmar Searle platted this street in 1887. He was born in Norway, and immigrated to St. Paul

in 1881 where he worked in the emigration department of a
railroad. Two years later, with Andrew E. Johnson, he
formed a company to aid emigrants settle in this country
and in one year alone, they arranged the sale of 25,000
acres of Minnesota land to new arrivals. Olaf is last
listed as a resident of Minneapolis in 1926.

SECOND STREET: Originally called Bench Street because of
its position halfway up the bluff, the name was changed in
1872. It is the second street from the river.

SELBY AVENUE: Reckoned as "industrious, economical, and
thrifty," Jeremiah W. Selby (1812-1855) traveled to St.
Paul in 1849 for his health, and purchased a forty-acre
farm on St. Anthony Hill where the St. Paul Cathedral now
stands. On this farm, for which he paid fifty dollars an
acre, Selby built a house and made a comfortable living
raising potatoes and garden vegetables. This street, part
of his homestead, was named in 1854.

SELMA LANE: Previously Grace Lane, the name was changed
in 1940.

SEMINARY AVENUE: In 1899, the Lutheran Seminary moved from
Robbinsdale, Minnesota, to the block at the west end of
this street. They constructed a large brick building for
their school facing on Englewood Avenue and Horton Park;
the following year this street was renamed Seminary Avenue.
In 1917, the Lutheran Seminary united with two others, and
formed the present-day Luther Theological Seminary on Como
Avenue in St. Anthony Park. In 1973, the site of the earlier
Seminary was bought by the St. Paul Housing and Redevelopment
Authority who demolished the old buildings and constructed a
public housing project for the elderly.

SEMINOLE AVENUE: Named in 1855 as one of a series of Indian
tribes, this street refers to the Seminole tribe who lived
in what is now Florida. Osceola was one of their famous
chiefs.

SEVENTH STREET: This was one of the original street names
of the city as it was platted in 1849. However, most of
West Seventh Street, outside of downtown, was first named
Fort Street, and it followed a very old path from Fort
Snelling to St. Paul, which accounts for its diagonal course.

SHAWMUT STREET: Shawmut is a village in Massachusetts, near
New Bedford. The name was applied in 1887 by the Union Land
Company.

SHELBY PLACE: Anna N. Shelby was the mother of Beriah and
Samuel Magoffin who owned property in the vicinity. She
was a granddaughter of Governor Isaac Shelby of Kentucky.

Since replaced by senior citizens housing, this was the Luther Seminary at the west end of Seminary Avenue.

SHELDON STREET: This street was named in 1881 for N. E. Sheldon, one of the developers. He was apparently never a resident of the city.

SHEPARD ROAD: The St. Paul City Council named this street in 1949 to honor George M. Shepard (1889-1973), chief engineer of the Department of Public Works from 1922-1927, and 1932-1956. During his years as chief engineer, he designed the Ford Parkway and Robert Street bridges, as well as the street that today bears his name.

Around 1900 there were strenuous efforts to extend the Mississippi River Boulevard along the river's shore from Fort Snelling to the High Bridge, but the project was finally abandoned in the 1930's, only to be replaced a decade later with Shepard Road.

HIGH BRIDGE, ST. PAUL

The wagon is traveling on top of the levee, a course later followed by Shepard Road. On the left are the "Bohemian Flats" a collection of squatters shanties long since replaced with the Northern States Power Plant.

SHERBURNE AVENUE: Remembered as "a real judge--calm, cool, decided, clear-headed, dignified," Moses Sherburne (1808-1868) was one of the developers of this street in 1857. He was born in Maine and came to St. Paul in 1853 as Judge of the United States District Court, appointed by President Franklin Pierce. He moved to Orono in Sherburne County (also named for him) in 1867.

SHERIDAN AVENUE: This street was named in 1891 by William Davern, most likely for Richard B. Sheridan (1751-1816), English playwright, orator and statesman. Davern, a one-time schoolteacher, would certainly have been aware of his writings.

SHERMAN STREET: Originally named Pine Street, it was renamed in 1872. It is said to honor William T. Sherman
(1820-1891), a Civil War general who conducted "the march
to the sea" through Georgia in 1864. There may also have
been a thought for Marshall Sherman (1822-1896), a St. Paul
painter who, in the course of the Civil War, became St.
Paul's first Medal of Honor winner.

SHERWOOD AVENUE: Orrin and Mary Sherwood platted this
street in 1887. He came to St. Paul about 1883 and engaged
in the real estate business until he moved to Minneapolis
in 1898.

SHIELDS AVENUE: General James Shields (1810-1879) was born
in Ireland, but immigrated to the United States when he was
sixteen where he earned his military rank in the Mexican
War. He was subsequently governor of Oregon Territory,
United States Senator from Illinois, and United States
Senator from Minnesota; he moved to California from which
state he served in the Civil War. He was later United States
Senator from Missouri. Shields platted this street in 1873.

SHORT STREET: Because the street was only a block long in
the original 1856 plat, this name was applied in a burst of
creativity.

SHORT LINE ROAD: Officially designated by the city in 1965,
the street takes its name from the adjacent railroad tracks
of the Chicago, Milwaukee, St. Paul and Pacific Railroad,
known locally as the Short Line because it runs only from
St. Paul to Minneapolis. Upon its construction in 1880,
this was one of the major commuter trains for the (then)
suburbs of the city. Stations were at Victoria Avenue
(Ridgewood), Marshall Avenue (Macalester Park), and at
Prior Avenue (Merriam and Union Parks). Trains ran every
half-hour.

SIBLEY STREET: Described as "a really good man--an honest
man--a moral man--an able man--an upright man--a worthy man--
a man whose name will long live in the history of the
Northwest" Henry Hastings Sibley (1811-1891) was Minnesota
Territory's delegate to the United States Congress when this
street was named in 1849. Sibley was born in Michigan and
subsequently became a partner in the American Fur Company.
He settled at Mendota in 1834, and the following year built
the first private stone dwelling in Minnesota. He moved to
St. Paul in 1862 where he built a fine house on Woodward
Street. Sibley was the first Governor of the state of
Minnesota and held many posts of responsibility and honor.
With Alexander Ramsey and Henry M. Rice, he was probably one
of the most influential of Minnesota pioneers.

SIDNEY STREET: Sidney D. Jackson was one of the developers
of this street about 1855. Jackson was apparently here

only a short time--from 1855 to 1857--when the depression hit and land values plummeted.

SIGURD STREET: Sigurd Bertelsen (1899-   ) was St. Paul Postmaster from 1955 to 1972 and previous to that, he was assistant land commissioner for the Northern Pacific Railway.   Bertelsen was well regarded and upon his retirement, the St. Paul City Council declared February 7, 1972, as Sig Bertelsen day. The name was applied to the street in 1969 by his friend, Grege Beckett, Plat Commissioner at the time.

SIMCOE STREET: Originally Hazel Street, the name was changed in 1872. There are a lake, county, and village in Ontario, Canada, with this name; perhaps one of these served as the inspiration. In any case, the name was short, and easy to pronounce and remember.

SIMON AVENUE: This street was named in 1904 by several parties from Stillwater, none of whom was named Simon.

SIMPSON STREET: Matthew Simpson (1811-1884) was, like Asbury and Hamline, a Bishop of the Methodist Episcopal Church. A one-time printer, law clerk, and physician, Simpson became a Methodist when he was twenty-five. Beginning as a circuit rider, he quickly advanced to become "the best known and most influential Methodist of his day in the United States; a counselor of statesmen and a public speaker of international repute." This street near Hamline University was named in 1881.

SIMS AVENUE: One possibility for the origin of this 1872 name might be John Sims, a carpenter from Canada who may have invested in the property. He died the following year on October 13 of typhoid fever, age twenty-nine.

SINNEN STREET: Bernard and Anna Sinnen platted this street as part of their farmstead in 1872. Bernard died in 1887; Anna in 1891. At least one descendant still lives in that general area.

SIXTH STREET: Platted in 1849 as the sixth street from the river, this is one of the original streets of St. Paul.

SKYWAY DRIVE: Previously Dilworth Avenue, the name was changed in 1957 at the instigation of one of the six residents of the street who found his mail going to Dilworth, Minnesota, instead of Dilworth Avenue.

SLOAN STREET: All the streets in this development were first names: Agnes, Tina, Mary, Emma. This street appears on the plat as Sloane, also a first name.

Sixth Street looking east from Wabasha Street about 1920.   The hill in the foreground marks the division between what used to be "Lowertown" with its steamboat landing at the foot of Jackson Street, and "Uppertown" with its steamboat landing at the foot of Eagle Street.

SMITH AVENUE: The first Smith Avenue was named in 1849 as part of Leech's Addition. It most likely honored Charles K. Smith, the Territorial Secretary who came here from Ohio in 1849 and returned to that state in 1851. Thirty-six years later, in 1887, with the building of the High Bridge, the city switched Forbes and Smith streets so that the long street extending over the High Bridge and into the West Side, which should have been Forbes, became instead, Smith Avenue. This change honored Robert Armstrong Smith (1827-1913), long-time Mayor of St. Paul. Born in Indiana, Smith came to Minnesota in 1853 as private secretary to his brother-in-law, Willis Gorman, Territorial Governor of Minnesota. He was subsequently Territorial Librarian, Treasurer of Ramsey County, City Alderman, state legislator, City Councilman, and Mayor from 1887-1892, 1894-1896, 1900-1908. He also served as Postmaster, and Ramsey County Commissioner.

SNELLING AVENUE: This street was named in 1856 for Colonel Josiah Snelling (1782-1828), commander of the military post

Looking north on Snelling Avenue from Randolph Avenue about
1940. The gas station and all the houses have been replaced
with a branch of the Twin City Federal Savings and Loan.
The children are on their way to Mattocks School.

which was given his name. Snelling Avenue follows roughly
an early path--and before that, an Indian trail--running
from Fort Snelling out to Little Canada. Today it follows
a section line. Few people know that mighty Snelling
Avenue, at its southern end, turns into a narrow country
road winding down a heavily wooded bluff to West Seventh
Street.

SNOWSHOE LANE: When confronted with a telephone call from
the city in 1956, requesting an immediate name for the
street on his plat, Dr. David French asked his secretary
for an idea. Noticing a pair of snowshoes on top of a
bookcase in the office, she suggested Snowshoe Lane, which
was conveyed to the city and accepted on the plat.

SPRING STREET: This obscure street was named in 1849,
most likely for the fact there was a spring bubbling from
the bluff.

SPRINGFIELD STREET: Applied in 1872, this street is most
likely named for the capitol city of Illinois. The developer, Charles Weide, was from that state.

SPRINGSIDE DRIVE: Previously Garden Avenue, the name was changed in 1948 as part of a general reorganization of street names within the area. The spring, from which the street takes its name, was a short distance below the intersection with Wildview Avenue.

SPRUCE STREET: Previously Baldwin Street, it was renamed. for the tree in 1872.

STANDISH STREET: Miles Standish (1584-1656), whose romance involving John Alden and Priscilla Mullens was recorded in Longfellow's poem The Courtship of Miles Standish, served as the inspiration for this 1885 street name.

STANFORD AVENUE: Originally extended as Grace Street (which name it retains east of Lexington Parkway), the new name was added in 1913. This was done, no doubt, at the behest of the developer of Macalester Villas who wished to have his streets renamed for colleges to coincide with those within adjacent Macalester Park.

STARKEY STREET: Originally part of Concord Street, the name was changed in 1883. Remembered as a prolific writer, a poet, and a good speaker, James Starkey (1818-1892) devised the sewer system for St. Paul in 1873. Born in England, he immigrated to America in 1849, and journeyed to St. Paul the following year. He was active in the Territorial government of the state, a captain in the local militia, a County Commissioner of Anoka County, and he also did extensive railroad surveying. In his later years, he was a member of the Plat Commission.

STATE STREET: Originally named Bertha Street, the name was changed in 1883. There is a well known State Street in Chicago.

STELLA STREET: This street was named in 1885 as part of St. Anthony Park.

STELLAR STREET: Stellar means, in the dictionary definition, "of or pertaining to the stars"--an ambitious name for this street so dubbed in the 1880's.

STERK ROAD: Adolph Sterk (1867-1953) was born in Freiburg, Germany, where, as a youth, he studied horticulture. Leaving Germany to avoid the draft, he immigrated to St. Paul in the 1890's, and worked for the Parks Department from about 1897 until his death. Over thirty years of his career with the Parks Department was in the capacity of principal clerk, with occasional stints as assistant super-intendent. He was married to Anna, daughter of Frederick Nusbaumer, a long-time Parks Superintendent. Before 1967, when this street within Como Park was officially named, the

Adolph Sterk in his Como Park office.

road was informally known as the Banana Valley Road from the custom of transporting banana plants from the greenhouse to the outdoors in the spring of the year.

STEVENS STREET: This street was platted in 1857 by William H. Stevens who apparently was never a resident of the state.

STEVENS STREET: The first white man to settle in Minneapolis, John H. Stevens (1820-1900) began farming immediately upon his arrival here. Gaining a reputation as an agricultural authority, Stevens was a charter member of the Hennepin County Agricultural Society and later, from 1893 to 1894, he served as President of the Minnesota State Agricultural Society, the organization responsible for naming this street within the State Fairgrounds. It is reported that, in 1853, Stevens and an associate imported the first full-blooded Devon cow and bull ever brought into Hennepin County; the animals cost them two thousand dollars.

STEWART AVENUE: Once called Bluff Street, the name was changed in 1872 to honor Dr. Jacob H. Stewart (1829-1884), three-term Mayor of St. Paul. Born in New York, he came to St. Paul in 1855 where, at various times, he served as Surgeon General of Minnesota, state senator, member of the St. Paul Board of Education, Postmaster, United States Congressman, and Surveyor General. He was noted in his younger years for his red hair and bright, gleeful, boyish air.

STICKNEY STREET: Alpheus Bede Stickney (1840-1916) was a lawyer and railroad official when this street was named in

1885. He is best known for his role as organizer and builder of the St. Paul Union Stock Yards and packing houses; and as President of the Chicago Great Western Railway Company.

STILLWATER AVENUE: There were a number of significant streets bearing this destination name in the early history of the city, but none of them remain. The present Stillwater Avenue is the result of renaming several streets; most of its length, before 1940, was known as Phalen Avenue.

STINCHFIELD STREET: This street was named in 1926 for J. H. Stinchfield, Secretary of the Bachman Realty Company. Henry Bachman bought about 250 acres in the area on the rumor that a bridge would be built across the Mississippi River at this point, thus greatly increasing the value of the land. When this did not happen, the land lay idle for many years until platted by the Bachman Realty Company. Henry Bachman, first of three generations of Richfield-Twin Cities florists, later moved to Long Beach, California, where he had an opportunity to purchase Signal Hill before oil was discovered on it. His wife insisted on his retirement, however, and the chance to make millions of dollars passed by.

STINSON STREET: James Stinson (1828-1917), one of the developers, named this street in 1883. A former resident of Hamilton, Ontario, he made twenty-four additions to the city of St. Paul, was one of the founders of Superior, Wisconsin, and invested heavily in Chicago canal lands. A man of immense wealth, he was probably the largest landowner in Ramsey County during the nineteenth century.

STONEBRIDGE BOULEVARD: Named in 1928, the street takes its name from the estate of Oliver Crosby which was entitled "Stonebridge." This estate originally occupied thirty-two acres between Jefferson and St. Clair avenues, Mississippi River Boulevard, and Mount Curve Boulevard. On the property was a very large, sumptuous, fifteen-room house built in 1915, a nine-car garage, numerous large outbuildings, and an artificial lake which drained riverward through a small ravine spanned by a stone bridge. This ravine, which is still perceptible, historically drained a marsh near the site of today's Groveland School, and was known as Finn's Glen, for William Finn, the first settler. The stone bridge still remains on the property.
    Oliver Crosby (1856-1922) owner of the estate, was a founder and president of American Hoist and Derrick Company. Upon Oliver's death, the estate went to his son, Frederick, who lived there for a time, but found the taxes insupportable. The house was offered to Governors Harold Stassen and Elmer Benson for a Governor's Mansion, but the money was not forthcoming. The house was let go for back taxes and finally demolished about 1952, a sad ending for a

Doomed "Stonebridge" at Christmas time.

beautiful estate. It is said the front gates from the
estate are at the Midway Parkway entrance to Como Park.

STRYKER AVENUE: John L. Stryker of New York state was one
of the developers of this street in 1855. Stryker was a
gentleman, that is to say, he did not have to work for a
living. John is not recorded as a resident of St. Paul,
but his son, John E. Stryker (1862-1940) moved to St. Paul
in 1887 as a lawyer.

STURGIS STREET: Charles E. Sturgis, his wife, Louisa, and
their son, William, platted this street in 1857. They
apparently never lived here.

SUBURBAN AVENUE: This street was named in 1882 as part of
Suburban Hills.

SUE STREET: James and Sue Fry, both of Bloomington,
Illinois, platted this street in 1886.

SUMAC STREET: Previously Bowdoin Street, the name was changed in 1940.

SUMMIT AVENUE: Platted in 1854, this elm-lined boulevard, St. Paul's showplace, was named because of its course along the top of the bluff. Summit, like other names indicating height, is a common street name.

SUMNER STREET: This is a fairly common place and family name, chosen here most likely for its faintly English sound. Other streets in this 1886 plat were named Norwich, Beverly, Salem, and Woodview.

SUNNY SLOPE LANE: Originally part of Itasca Street, the name was changed in 1955 at the request of the residents, to avoid confusion between the west and east segments of Itasca Street which were widely separated.

SUPERIOR STREET: This street was named in 1851 for the Great Lake. Other names given at this time were St. Clair, Michigan, Ontario, Erie, and Huron.

SUPORNICK LANE: Lieutenant David Supornick was killed in the Normandy invasion in 1944, during World War II. As a testimonial to all the United States soldiers killed in that war, Supornick's name was offered by his brother-in-law, Sidney Goff, secretary of the Housing and Redevelopment Authority who platted this public housing project in 1951.

SURREY AVENUE: Previously Van Buren Place, the name was changed in 1940.

SUSAN AVENUE: Susan was the daughter of Leonard Bisanz, one of the brothers who developed the area in 1951.

SYCAMORE STREET: This street was named for the tree in 1856.

SYLVAN STREET: Sylvan means abounding in woods, groves, or trees. As such it was a popular name even though this particular area may not have been so distinguished when this street was named in 1857.

SYNDICATE STREET: The St. Paul Real Estate Syndicate was the developer of this area in 1882.

T

TAINTER AVENUE: Andrew Tainter (1823-1899) and his wife, Bertha, were investors in St. Anthony Park when this street was named in 1885. Born in Salina, New York, Tainter settled at Menomonie, Wisconsin, in 1846 where he later became a partner with John H. Knapp in what developed into one of the largest lumbering concerns in the world. He was an investor in St. Anthony Park, but never lived in Minnesota.

TATUM STREET: Samuel C. Tatum and his wife Eleanor of Cincinnati, Ohio, were partners with Hannah Tatum of Philadelphia in developing this Midway Heights Addition in 1885. They invested in this property at the instigation of Pennock Pusey, a real estate dealer in St. Paul.

TAYLOR AVENUE: William G. and Charlotte F. Taylor owned property in the vicinity of this street named in 1881. The following year, they platted property west of Snelling Avenue, and Charlotte Street was also named. Neither of the Taylors, who sold out their property six years later, was a resident of the city.

TELL STREET: Named by Adam Gotzian in 1883, this is probably a personal name.

TEMPERANCE STREET: One of downtown's most obscure avenues, Temperance Street was named in 1851 for the virtue of abstaining from alcoholic beverages. At this early date, temperance was a spirited question and the first society for that purpose had been organized in St. Paul only three years previous. It is said that, in its later years, the street was graced by a saloon.

TEMPLE COURT: A street name applied in 1890, the temple area (known as the Inns of Court) is an ancient district of London in which lawyers have traditionally lived and studied.

TENTH STREET: The first complete high school building in the city was constructed at Tenth and Minnesota streets in 1883. With its twenty-five teachers and 500 pupils, the building

was located in what was then a residential area of the city.
Tenth Street itself was named in 1850.

TERRACE STREET: Named in 1885, this street takes its name
from the fact it runs along the hillside above what was
once the course of Trout Brook.

TERRITORIAL ROAD: Congress appropriated money to the War
Department in 1850 for the construction of a road from
Point Douglas, via Cottage Grove, Red Rock, St. Paul and
the Falls of St. Anthony, to Fort Ripley. Then, as now,
good roads were considered a necessary part of national
defense. Except for an alley mentioned under Van Buren
Avenue, all that remains of this early road between the
Twin Cities can be found in the few blocks now labeled as
Territorial Road.

TEWANNA PLACE: In keeping with some of the other street
names within the Beaver Lake Heights Addition platted in
1917, this is quite possibly a Chippewa word.

THERESA PLACE: Theresa Eisenmenger was a close friend of
the Bohland family when they platted this street in 1927;
she may have been the inspiration for the name.

THIRD STREET: Named in 1849, this is one of the original
street names of St. Paul. The original townsite began
numbering with Third Street; the second street from the
river was Bench Street, and the street next to the river
was Water Street. The present Third Street was extended
from downtown, while the original portion has been renamed
as Kellogg Boulevard.

THIRTEENTH STREET: William Dahl, a stationer born in
England, immigrated to St. Paul in 1851. Seven years later,
when Minnesota became a state, Dahl built a frame house at
136 Thirteenth Street. His house remains today as, I
believe, the only private single dwelling left in the downtown area. In the nineteenth century, Williams's son,
Edward, picked chestnuts where the state capitol now stands;
today the 117 year old Dahl house is owned by the state who
may demolish or remove it within the year.

THOMAS AVENUE: This street was named in 1856 for Thomas
Stinson, the developer, through his son and agent, James
Stinson. Thomas, a man of great wealth, lived in Hamilton,
Ontario, Canada. Upon his death March 14, 1864, he had
$45,000 worth of property in Ramsey County. His son James
of Chicago continued the family investments here, and
became probably the largest property owner in Ramsey County
during the nineteenth century.

THOMPSON STREET: Originally part of Forbes Avenue, the
name was changed in 1887. The new name may have honored
Horace Thompson, an influential banker and civic leader.

Looking south on Marion Street toward Thomas Avenue, about 1925.
Scheffer School, since demolished, is pictured on the left.

THORN STREET: Previously Richmond Avenue, the name was changed in 1872.

THURE AVENUE: Thure A. Johnson (1886-1972) platted this street in 1923. Born in Sweden, Johnson came to St. Paul as a young man where he worked as a carpenter and contractor. His name was pronounced "Thurey."

TILSEN AVENUE: Edward N. Tilsen (1892-   ) is the home building contractor and developer responsible for over 2000 "Tilsenbilt" homes. He was born in Russia, but immigrated to St. Paul in the 1930's, and named this street in 1955.

TIMBERLAKE ROAD: This street was added to the city in 1950 as part of the McDonough public housing project. C. Jerome Timberlake (1923-1944) was a Lieutenant in the United States Army, killed in the Battle of the Bulge. His name was suggested by one of the veterans' associations. John J. McDonough (1895-1962) for whom the housing project was named, was Mayor of St. Paul from 1940-1948.

TOPIC LANE: Previously part of McAfee Street, the name was changed in 1955.

TOPPING STREET: This street was platted in 1883 as part of the Foundry Addition because of its proximity to the St. Paul Foundry Company of which Herbert W. Topping (1850-1915) was General Manager. Born in England, Topping came to Minnesota in 1870. He was an alderman, and later President of the Park Board.

TORONTO STREET: A. Vance Brown, the developer of this street in 1856, was a native of Canada. He is listed as a resident here in 1860, but he apparently did not remain long.

TOTEM ROAD: Previously part of Burlington Avenue, the name was changed in 1948 as part of a general reorganization of street names within the area. On this street is a Ramsey County residential treatment facility known as Boys Totem Town. This name, which has been in use for at least thirty years, is derived from the totem poles, carved by the boys, that grace the grounds. The institution moved to his location about 1913 as a boy's farm and industrial school for habitual truants and incorrigibles.

TOWER STREET: Officially known as the McKnight Road Standpipe, the water tower at the south end of this street was built in 1955, one year before the street was named.

TRUXTON STREET: This street was named in 1873 for Thomas Truxton (1755-1822) a naval officer born on Long Island. An active officer in the American Revolution, Truxton first went to sea at age twelve, and became a ship commander when he was twenty. Other streets named in this plat were for Matthew Maury, Stephen Decatur, James Lawrence, and Edward Preble, all famous naval officers of the early nineteenth century.

TURNER STREET: This street was quite possibly named for William F. and Hamlin Turner. Hamlin was in Minneapolis real estate and probably owned shares in the St. Anthony Park Company; his brother William, the first settler in Price County, Wisconsin, was a sometime logging contractor, and proprietor of the hotel in Fifield.

TUSCARORA AVENUE: The Tuscarora Indian tribe prompted this street name in 1881. An adjacent street, since renamed Watson, was originally Iroquois.

TWELFTH STREET: This, the twelfth street from the river, was named in 1852.

U

UNDERWOOD STREET: This street within the State Fairgrounds, named by the Minnesota State Agricultural Society, honors Joseph Merritt Underwood (1844-1922) who was active in the management of the Society and served as its President in 1910. Underwood, born in Palmyra, New York, came to Minnesota shortly after the Civil War, settling in Lake City as a farmer.

UNIVERSITY AVENUE: Because this street first ran between the University of Minnesota and Hamline University, it was given its name in 1874. The establishment of the Minnesota Transfer Yards, however, blocked the course of the street, and it was necessary to shift the eastern end of the avenue one-half mile further south. Thus Melrose Avenue assumed the name of University Avenue, and the original University Avenue became Minnehaha Avenue.

UPLAND AVENUE: Height is the single most popular element in street names, hence the appeal of this common name applied here in 1888.

UPPER AFTON ROAD: Constructed before the Civil War, this county road from St. Paul ran along the top of the bluffs toward Afton on the St. Croix River.

UPPER ST. DENNIS ROAD: Den E. Lane (1881-1952) was one of the most active St. Paul real estate men in the 1920's and 1930's, and a foremost developer in Highland Park. Born in Ireland, Lane moved to St. Paul as a child, and began his real estate ventures when yet a student at St. Thomas College. Known as "The Own Your Home Man," Lane estimated that, in the 1920's, he had designed, laid out, and named fifty percent of the St. Paul streets in the preceding decade. By 1925, he had handled more than ten thousand property transactions. This street, platted in 1945, was named for his patron saint, Dennis.

URBAN PLACE: Previously Lizzie Street, the name was changed in 1905. The word urban implies a city or town; this street occurs in the Suburban Hills addition. One of St.

Paul's oldest elm trees, more than 102 years old, was at 155 Urban Place. Marked with an historic marker, the tree died from Dutch Elm disease, and had to be removed in 1974.

UTICA AVENUE: Originally Wabasso Avenue, the name was changed in 1940.

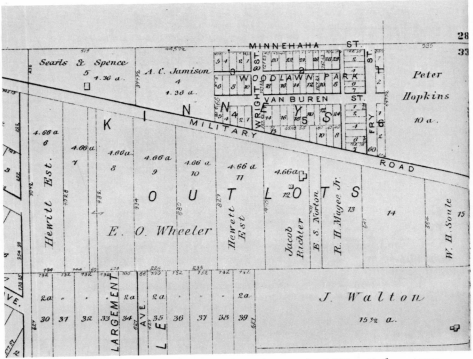

The course of the old military road as it was in 1886. Today a portion of the road remains as a diagonal alley between Blair, Aldine, Wheeler, and Van Buren streets.

VALENTINE AVENUE: Platted as Pierce Street in 1885, the name was changed in 1940 to avoid duplication.

VALLEY STREET: This street was platted in 1856, and named for the fact it used to come down the hill from Jackson Street, parallel to Mt. Airy Street.

VALLEY SIDE DRIVE: This street was named in 1970 because, the proprietor felt, it just sounded nice.

VALLEY VIEW PLACE: The view down into the Mississippi River valley prompted this street name in 1965.

VAN BUREN AVENUE: Martin Van Buren (1782-1862) was the eighth President of the United States. This street took his name in 1871. Within the block bounded by Blair, Van Buren, Wheeler, and Aldine streets, there is a diagonal alley which follows the course of the early territorial road running from St. Paul to St. Anthony (now southeast Minneapolis). This short stretch of alley is one of the few remnants of the first road between the two cities.

VAN DYKE STREET: James W. Van Dyke was the developer of this property in 1887. Unmarried at the time, a carpenter by profession, he was listed as a resident of the city only from 1887 to 1889.

VAN SLYKE AVENUE: Recalled as a man who made two blades of grass grow where there was but one, William A. Van Slyke (1833-1910) was called the founder of our present park system because of his efforts on the City Council as Chairman of the Committee on Parks. Born in New York state, he moved to St. Paul in 1854 as a store clerk; by 1857 the business was his. Active in many public affairs, he was "the man above all other men who has transformed our dirty, sombre, dark, forbidding parks into gems of loveliness." His name was selected for this street because of its proximity to Como Park.

VANCE STREET: Alexander Vance Brown was a real estate speculator during the 1850's in this area.

VANDALIA STREET: This was a popular and common name when the street was platted in 1881.

VERNON STREET: Originally called Witherspoon Avenue, the name was changed in 1890. George H. Vernon, a lawyer, developed some property near St. Clair and Snelling avenues; perhaps his name was the source.

VICTORIA STREET: Victoria was Queen of England when this street was named in 1871 by a former British subject, John Wann.

VIEW STREET: This street was named in 1857, apparently for the pleasant associations of the word, since there does not seem to be any striking view on the street.

VILLARD COURT: Henry Villard (1835-1900) was a journalist, railway promoter, and financier when this street was platted as part of Hiawatha Park in 1890. Born in Germany, he came to the United States at age eighteen where he studied law and edited a newspaper in Illinois. For the following fifteen years, he worked as a journalist but one of his investigations led him into a career as railroad promoter. He became President of the Northern Pacific Railroad in 1881 and completed the line to the west coast in 1883, making it a transcontinental railroad, a feat for which he is honored by this street name.

VIRGINIA STREET: State names are always popular; this one was applied in 1854.

VISTA AVENUE: This name was chosen in 1881 to give, no doubt, the suggestion of a striking view.

WABASH AVENUE: The river which forms the border between Illinois and Indiana most likely prompted this street name in 1881.

WABASHA STREET: One of the original street names of St. Paul, it was assigned in 1849. Wabasha was the name of three hereditary Sioux or Dakota Indian chiefs. The first Wabasha ruled his area under the French, and after 1759, the British. His son, Wabasha the second, succeeded about the time of the American Revolution--in which he went East to fight on the side of the British. His village stood near the town of Rolling Stone in Winona County. The third Wabasha succeeded about 1837, negotiated treaties with the whites, fought in the Sioux Uprising, and died on an Indian reservation in Nebraska in 1876. All three Indians were highly respected men.

WACOUTA STREET: This was one of the first street names of the city, named in 1849 for Wacouta, an Indian chief and the son of Red Wing. Wacouta became chief just as the whites were coming into the state in numbers, and he was forced into signing unwise land treaties and joining in the Sioux Uprising. Like Wabasha, he died on the Santee Indian reservation in Nebraska.

WADENA AVENUE: Previously Arlington Avenue, the name was changed in 1940 to avoid duplication.

WAGENER STREET: John and Susan Wagener platted this street in 1886. He came to St. Paul in 1873 where he had a coal, wood, and brick store in this area. Active in public affairs, he served as Ramsey County Commissioner. Their son of the same name was several times Sheriff of Ramsey County. A native of Luxembourg, John died in 1888. Susan, a native of Alsace-Lorraine, died in 1895.

WAKEFIELD AVENUE: Originally called Birch Street, the name was changed in 1892 to honor William Wakefield (1825-1906). Born in Rhode Island, he moved to St. Paul in 1856 where he worked in the dry goods business. In 1860 he purchased four acres on Dayton's Bluff for about $300; today this property lies between Wakefield, Forest, Cypress and Wilson streets. On his land he built a house and planted trees making it, as a contemporary said: "a very lovely and desirable home" and "one of the beautiful residences of the city." The house remains at 963 Wakefield Avenue, but the estate, once named "What Cheer Lawn," has long since been subdivided into building lots.

WALES STREET: Originally named Warren Street, the name was changed in 1940.

WALL STREET: Designated Rosabel Street in 1849, one of the first and most historic streets of the city, the name was changed in 1970 at the request of the North Central Life Insurance Company. At the time, the Company had purchased the Wall Street Mutual Fund, and they wished to have a Wall Street address to use with this mutual fund.

WALNUT STREET: It is said a grove of walnut trees standing where St. Luke's Hospital is today prompted this name in 1849.

WALSH STREET: Vincent D. Walsh was one of the developers of this street in 1872. Living in New Orleans, Louisiana, he made substantial investments in St. Paul real estate, and his name appears on many plats and deeds. At his death in 1899, he left $135,670 worth of property in Ramsey County.

WANDA STREET: Previously Highland Street, the name was changed in 1940 to avoid duplication.

WARBLER LANE: This street was so named, in 1970, because as the developer put it, the name just sounded nice.

WARNER ROAD: The City Council named this road in 1937 for Richmond Perez Warner (1871-1936), chairman of the St. Paul Port Authority and the Upper Mississippi and St. Croix River Improvement Commission. Born in St. Paul, he was educated at home and abroad. Beginning as a stock clerk with a shoe company, he worked his way up to become Vice-President of Griggs, Cooper, and Company. Warner was deeply committed to the improvement of the upper Mississippi River as a major transportation route, with the nine-foot channel one of his goals. Upon his death, the City Hall flag was flown at half-mast for fifteen days. Anne Warner French, a well-known author around the turn of the century, was Richmond's sister.

WARREN STREET: The city of St. Paul named this street in 1959, most likely for Henry E. (Ned) Warren (1893-1965), City Councilman and Public Safety Commissioner of St. Paul in 1934 and 1935 when he was instrumental in ridding the

THE LAY OF NINA CLIFFORD

The windows are grimy and covered with dust
    In that old house under the hill
The door hinges rusty, the lock is bust
    The spider webs cover it still
No longer do gay lights their welcome convey
    Inviting the wayfarer in
To choose from the bevy, his favorite lay
    To dally a while and sin.

Gone are the sofas and plush covered chairs
    From the parlor once happy and bright
No longer do douche pans in bedrooms upstairs
    Clank busily all thru the night
No more do fat burghers play and carouse
    And jounce pretty blonds on their backs
For Nina is dead and her once famous house
    Is sold to pay up the back tax.

They're widening the street so they're tearing it down
    They're tearing its timbers apart
The whorehouse that once was the pride of the town
    Soon won't be worth more than a fart
Its stone they are taking the morgue to repair
    A purpose appropriate -- true
For many a stiff has been lain in them both
    Even as me and you.

Those who wish may clip out this poem to protect minors and other innocents of all ages. There is nothing printed on the reverse side.

city of gangsters. Born in Canada, he moved to St. Paul as a boy where he graduated from Central High School. He entered the automobile sales business in 1918, and continued in that occupation the rest of his life, with the exception of his years on the City Council.

WARWICK STREET: William and Mary Brimhall platted this street in 1886. Warwick is a county and city in England; the other English street names in this vicinity were: Berkeley (now Palace), Rothley (Jefferson), and Wilford (Stanford).

WASECA STREET: Originally Sophia Street, the name was changed in 1883. Waseca is a Sioux word meaning fertile land.

WASHINGTON STREET: This street was named in 1849 for George Washington, first President of the United States. Eighty years later, the street was infamous as the address of Nina Clifford's house.

Located at 147 South Washington Street near the Bucket of Blood saloon, this was the brothel of St. Paul's most famous madam, Nina Clifford. Built in 1888, it was torn down in 1937, the victim of overdue taxes and poor maintenance. Upon that occasion, St. Paul Mayor Larry Hodgson (see Larry Ho Drive) is said to have written "The Lay of Nina Clifford."

WATER STREET: A common name among river towns, it was applied here in 1858. One of the city engineers recalls a dream whereby Water Street in Duluth was flooded out. That city appealed to St. Paul, and this engineer was assigned to move St. Paul's Water Street to Duluth.

WATERLOO STREET: Recalling the defeat of Napoleon, this name was given in 1885.

WATSON AVENUE: John J. and Joanna B. Watson platted this street in 1886. A native of Ulster County, New York, Watson left school at age eleven, subsequently learned the trade of watchmaker and jeweler, and later worked as a clerk. In 1869, he moved to Chicago where he worked for a fire insurance company. The Chicago fire of 1871 destroyed the company, and in 1875 he came to St. Paul. Four years later he began his many real estate investments, including the development of Lexington Park. Watson is said to have originated the idea of selling houses on the installment plan and he is remembered as a man of enterprise and boldness. He was born in 1850 and died in 1925.

WAUKON AVENUE: Applied in 1917, this is a Chippewa word of indefinite meaning.

WAVERLY PLACE: William H. Jarvis of St. Paul named this street in 1851, probably for the village of Waverly in his native New York state. In the 1880's, this street was in an area of fine homes and mansions.

WAYZATA STREET: Both Wayzata and Litchfield, Minnesota, were stops along the St. Paul and Pacific Railroad in 1872 when this street was named.

WEBSTER STREET: Originally named Second Street in 1856, the name was changed in 1872. It most likely commemorated Daniel Webster (1782-1852), American statesman and orator.

WEIDE STREET: Charles A. B. Weide (1833-1892) was a real estate dealer when this street was named in 1872. Born in Germany, Weide came to the United States with his parents, moving to St. Paul in 1853 where he worked in a store on Third Street. He later took up real estate in which he did well and was, in his own words, "the happiest man in the state."

WELLESLEY AVENUE: Platted as Sloan and Lansing streets, the name was changed in 1913. This was done, no doubt, at the behest of the developer of Macalester Villas who wished to have his streets renamed as colleges to coincide with those within Macalester Park.

WELLS STREET: Like several streets in this addition, the origin of this name is uncertain. Applied in 1872, it could refer to George Wells, a bus driver for Cook's St. Paul Omnibus Company. Built into a hillside between Greenbrier and Walsh streets, Wells is divided into a lower east-bound lane and an upper west-bound lane. With one lane twenty-four feet above the other, it is no place for a U-turn.

WESTERN AVENUE: This was the westernmost street on its 1854 plat.

WESTMINSTER STREET: John E. Warren named this street in 1853, most likely for Westminster, London, the site of Westminster Abbey.
  To the west of Westminster Street and south of York Avenue, where the railroad yards now stand, was the home of Edmund Rice. Entitled "Trout Brook Farm" and encompassing forty-five acres, the estate had a plum orchard, summer house,

RES. OF EDMUND RICE ESQ.

"Trout Brook Farm"

ice house, barn, and a large mansion built in 1862 with eight bedrooms and three bathrooms. Trout Brook, running through the grounds, was dammed to create an artificial lake. Financially hard-pressed, Rice sold his estate to the railroad in 1883, and the grounds and house were destroyed.

WEST SHORE DRIVE: Following the west shore of Lake Phalen, this street was named by the city in 1967.

WEYMOUTH STREET: The Union Land Company borrowed this name from the village in Massachusetts and applied it here in 1887.

WHEELER STREET: One source records Everett P. Wheeler, a well-known New York lawyer as the cause of this name. Another possibility is Rush B. Wheeler (1844-1930), a prominent real estate man in St. Paul. Rush was born in New York state, graduated from Yale University, and came to Austin, Minnesota, where he studied law with his brother. He moved to St. Paul in 1883 and was subsequently active in the Chamber of Commerce, Real Estate Board, and the Y.M.C.A.

WHEELOCK PARKWAY: Joseph Albert Wheelock (1831-1906) was born in Nova Scotia, and came to St. Paul in 1850 searching for better health. Eleven years later he founded the St. Paul Pioneer Press, remaining its editor until the end of his life. Active in civic affairs and politics, Wheelock was Postmaster of St. Paul for five years, and in 1893 he

Looking northeast on Wheelock Parkway from Cohansey Street about 1915. The two houses to the left of the automobile remain at 1501 Western Avenue and 1458 Cumberland Street.

was appointed President of the St. Paul Park Board, a position he held for thirteen years. Named three years after his death, this parkway which links Lakes Como and Phalen, commemorates Wheelock's prodigious efforts to complete the St. Paul park system.

WHITALL STREET: Remembered for her "bright, beautiful countenance with black hair and black eyes," Matilda Whitall (1827-1906) was the wife of Henry M. Rice, and sister-in-law to the developer, Edmund Rice. Born in Rome, New York, Matilda moved to Richmond, Virginia, when she was seven. She met Henry Rice in Washington, D.C., where she was attending school and later married him in 1849.

WHITE BEAR AVENUE: Laid out as a county road between Hudson Road and Larpenteur Avenue in 1886, the name was changed to White Bear Avenue two years later.

WILDER STREET: Helen M. Wilder (1835-1915) was the second wife of John L. Merriam, the developer of this street in 1882. Her brother, Amherst H. Wilder (1828-1894), was a one-time business partner of the Merriams. Born in Vermont, Amherst moved to St. Paul about 1859 where he worked with several different firms in the transportation of goods, including the railroads. He was very active in the business community, amassing a good deal of money in the process, and several charitable institutions throughout St. Paul bear his name.

WILDVIEW AVENUE: Previously Springfield Avenue, the name was changed in 1940 to avoid duplication.

WILKIN STREET: Known as the "Little Captain" because of his small stature, Alexander Wilkin (1820-1864) was born in Orange County, New York, where he studied law with his father. After earning the rank of captain in the Mexican War, he moved to St. Paul where he practiced law and dabbled in real estate, naming this street in 1849. He was United States Marshal for Minnesota, a founder of the St. Paul Companies, and later fought in the Civil War where he was killed. There is also a Minnesota county named for him.

WILLIAM TELL ROAD: The mother of the developer was born in Switzerland making this an appropriate street name in his Swiss Meadows Addition.

WILLIAMS STREET: Brook B. Williams was one of the developers of this street in 1857. Williams is presently a ghost street, unmarked, unused, and largely forgotten. The hill upon which the street runs is slowly being cut away for the gravel underneath.

The first burials in the city were made here when it was known as Oak Hill. In the 1870's, the Broadway-Mississippi streetcar line ended here, and the hill was a

"Swedish Castle" on Williams Hill at the corner of Williams and Pine Streets. Built in 1880 by Andrew M. Carlsen, a St. Paul patent attorney, the thirty-seven room house offered accommodations to newly arrived Scandinavian immigrants.

favorite picnic spot. During the following decade there were houses built on the hill, not the expensive mansions reported in some accounts, but smaller single family dwellings and larger boarding houses and apartments. In the early 1900's the railroad began actively acquiring the land and houses, planning to level the hill and build more shops. By the first World War most of the homes were gone, although a few lasted into the 1950's.

This hill, now known as Williams Hill, is one of the historic vantage points of the city, and notwithstanding its encirclement by the railroad and the freeway, deserves a better use.

WILLIUS STREET: Originally platted as College Street in 1852, the name was changed in 1872 to avoid duplication. Ferdinand Willius (1830-1916) and his brother, Gustav (1831-1924) were born in Germany and immigrated to St. Paul in the 1850's where they opened a bank which prospered under several names in the succeeding years. Ferdinand was a member of the City Council at the time the street name was changed. Both brothers were considered "cool, careful, calculating, cautious, conservative, industrious, and financially shrewd." They were also wealthy.

WILMOT AVENUE: At one time Caulfield Avenue, the name was changed in 1940.

WILSHIRE PLACE: Formerly River Street, the name was changed in 1940.

WILSON AVENUE: Previously Hudson Avenue, the name was changed in 1940 to avoid confusion with Hudson Road.

WINCHELL STREET: Phillip D. Winchell platted this street in 1888 with his wife, Martha. A carpenter on the West Side, Phillip died in 1912.

WINDMILL STREET: Born in Baden, Germany, Michael Strub (1817-1897) traveled to Minnesota in 1857 by way of Sandusky, Ohio. He lived at Sixth and John streets for a while, then purchased a farm between the present-day limits of West-minster and Windmill, Arlington and Clear avenues. When the railroad dissected his farm, he platted the east half in 1888. The surveyor indicated to Michael that he needed some street names; Michael replied that he didn't care, so the surveyor picked Strub (now Clear Avenue), and Residence Street (since vacated) because it ran by the house. The surveyor must also have looked around and seen a windmill, prompting that street name. The one-and-a-half story farm house stood on what is now the west bank of Interstate Highway 35E, just south of Arlington Avenue. When Michael and his wife Katherina died, the remainder of the farm was subdivided in 1926.

WINIFRED STREET: Originally Harriet Street, the name was changed in 1876 to signify the daughter of William P. Murray, President of the City Council at this time. She married Richard Demming, was widowed about 1894, taught school, and lived in the city until 1916 when her name was no longer listed in the city directory.

WINNIPEG AVENUE: The "dean of St. Paul real estate men," Robert P. Lewis (1835-1934) named this street in 1882. He came to St. Paul from Pennsylvania in 1859 as a law school graduate, and after the Civil War he went into real estate. Manitoba and Winnipeg streets were named together.

WINONA STREET: Once named Julia Street, the name was changed in 1883. Winona is a Sioux word meaning first-born daughter. There is a county by this name in Minnesota.

WINSLOW AVENUE: Remembered as a man who "measured his words as a clerk measures molasses in cold weather," James M. Winslow (1810-1885) was one of the developers of this street in 1855. Born in the East, he ran a large stagecoach business in Vermont before coming to St. Paul in 1852. Here he built several hotels, all of which bore his name, plus the Winslow Mill on Trout Brook. He also introduced telegraph service to the city, running a line from Dubuque to St. Paul. He later moved to California, but his body was returned to Oakland Cemetery for burial.

WINSTON STREET: This was platted in 1885 by Mary and Edgar C. Long who lived near Hewitt and Snelling avenues. The city directory for that year lists Eunice Winston as boarding with them; she may have been a sister or some other relative.

WINTER STREET: While this street was named in 1858 for the season and remains under its original name, a nearby Summer Street has since been changed to Sherburne Avenue.

WINTHROP STREET: The Union Land Company borrowed this name from a town near Boston, and applied it here in 1888.

WISCONSIN AVENUE: This street was named for the state in 1876.

WITHAM AVENUE: Previously Wilder Avenue, the name was changed in 1888.

WOOD STREET: "A large man, with large brain, and large heart, and large sympathies," Edward H. Wood (1836-1907), a native of Kentucky, traveled to St. Paul in 1856 where he helped survey building lots around Como Lake. He subsequently engaged in real estate speculation, was admitted to the Bar in 1860, served in the Civil War, and settled on the West Side in 1867.

WOODBRIDGE STREET: This street was named in 1876 most
likely for the sound of the word; at any rate I could find
no evidence of a bridge in the area.

WOODBURY STREET: Dwight Woodbury (1800-1884) owned extensive property in the area and platted Woodbury and Case's
Addition here in 1874. Born in Charlton, Massachusetts,
he moved to Minnesota in 1855 and settled in the Anoka area
where he was an active community leader.

WOODCREST DRIVE: This street was named in 1964 as part of
the Bacchus St. Paul Hills Addition.

WOODLAWN AVENUE: Applied here in 1913, wood is always a
popular component of place and street names, implying trees,
shade, and the like.

WOODWARD STREET: Now covered with railroad tracks and ware-
houses, Woodward Street was once, in the 1880's, a most
exclusive address. Location of the Thompson, Sibley, and
Wilder mansions, each with its own large grounds and extensive private driveways, the street had at its far end
picturesque Trout Brook. The whole area, entirely residential at that time, was known as Lower Town. Absolutely nothing of it remains today, except perhaps the brick streets.
Woodward is named for an avenue in Detroit, Henry Sibley's
birthplace.

WORCESTER AVENUE: Worcester, a county of England, prompted
this street name in 1912.

WORDSWORTH AVENUE: William Davern, who named this street
in 1891, was a one-time school teacher well acquainted with
the poetry of William Wordsworth (1770-1850).

WRIGHT AVENUE: This street within the State Fairgrounds
honors Kindy C. Wright, architect for many of the buildings
presently gracing the Fairgrounds. Born in St. Paul in
1893, Wright began an association with the Fair in 1933
that continues to this day. In his early years with the
Fair he supervised the many Emergency Relief Administration
(ERA) and Works Progress Administration (WPA) building pro-
jects on the Fairgrounds. Among these were the Conservation
Building (now the Natural Resources Building) built by the
ERA in 1934, the Horse Barn and Poultry Buildings in 1937,
the half-mile dirt track in 1939, and the 4-H Buildings--
for which Wright personally obtained the funding from the
WPA--in 1939. Wright's private firm also designed, in the
late 1940's and early 1950's, the Agriculture Building,
the Food Building, and the Hippodrome (now the Coliseum).

WYCLIFF STREET: Part of St. Anthony Park, this street was
named in 1885 for John Wycliff (1320?-1384), an English
religious scholar who, by his criticism of the Roman
Catholic Church, sowed the seeds of the later Reformation.

__WYNNE AVENUE__: Platted west of Fairview Avenue in 1885 as part of St. Anthony Park, this street now exists only east of Fairview Avenue.

__WYOMING STREET__: Originally Judith Street, the name was changed in 1883 to acknowledge the state.

YORK AVENUE: Platted as Douglas Street, the name was changed in 1872. The present name is very common and was chosen probably because it was short, easy to pronounce and remember.

YORKSHIRE AVENUE: This was named in 1948 as part of Hampshire Park. Both Yorkshire and Hampshire are counties in England; the reason for their selection is not recalled.

YOUNG STREET: John Young, the developer, owned six and a half acres in the vicinity when this street was named in 1887.

YOUNGMAN AVENUE: Christopher W. Youngman, a native of Indiana, named this street in 1886. He moved to St. Paul about 1882 where he first managed a piano and organ store downtown. Later he went into the real estate business and bought the forty-acre West Seventh Street stone quarries.

INDEX

Current street names appear in alphabetical sequence within the text. They are not indexed here.

*Current street names appear in alphabetical sequence within
the text. They are not indexed here.*

Current street names appear in alphabetical sequence within the text. They are not indexed here.

Current street names appear in alphabetical sequence within the text. They are not indexed here.

*Current street names appear in alphabetical sequence within
the text. They are not indexed here.*

*Current street names appear in alphabetical sequence within
the text. They are not indexed here.*

Current street names appear in alphabetical sequence within the text. They are not indexed here.

Current street names appear in alphabetical sequence within the text. They are not indexed here.

acknowledgements

This book is the result of an inordinate amount of work by the author, assisted by a few very good friends. It is, in every way, a personal endeavor; no institutions were involved in the research, writing, editing, publishing, or sale of the volume. The few good friends are:

Janet Moosbrugger, who edited the book and fortified the author with large doses of her considerable intelligence, unfailing wit, and reassuring enthusiasm.

James Taylor Dunn, who sparked my interest in local history over a decade ago, read this manuscript, as he has all my writings, with concern for its content and style.

Catherine Perusse, who not only typed the manuscript several times with extraordinary care and accuracy, but also arranged the type so it is attractive and uniform throughout the book.

Naomi Jefferson, who, with characteristic verve and energy, skilfully laid out this book and designed its very appealing cover.

Mary Ann, my wife, who did the indexing, proofreading, errand running, and other necessary tasks.

John A. Dougherty, who, careful scholar that he is, contributed numerous notes and references on the street names gathered in the course of his own research.

Jim Sazevich, "the Black Russian," who, without reservation, freely shared his information on the houses and streets of the East Side.

Michael Klassen, aide in the vault of the Department of Public Works, who was always cheerful and helpful without once questioning (although I'm sure he must have wondered) the value of my research.

Alfred Lischke, retired from the Department of Public Works, who was always willing to call upon his memory and files for some scrap of information I needed.

Bonnie Wilson, who made many useful suggestions about the photographs.

Christopher and Amy, my children, who spent many hours deprived of my good company.

picture credits

The photographs used in the frontispiece, and on pages 4,
15, 27, 31, 43, 46, 53, 59, 60, 62, 74, 75, 76, 82, 87,
101, 104, 110, 111, 115, 122, 128, 135, 136, 139, 140,
142, 144, 149, 159, 161, 162, and 164 are from the extensive and well cataloged collection of the Audio-Visual
Library of the Minnesota Historical Society.

The photographs on pages 80 and 84 are from the Public
Relations section of the St. Paul Department of Public Works.

The advertisements reproduced on pages 21, 40, 52, and 165
are from the first directory ever published in St. Paul:
*Business Directory for the City of St. Paul, Minnesota
Territory*, August 1, 1856. St. Paul: Goodrich & Somers,
Printers, Pioneer and Democrat Office, 1856. A copy of this
rare directory is in the Library of the Minnesota Historical
Society.

The portrait of Maria Bates Dayton on page 9 is from the:
History of the City of Minneapolis, Minnesota. Isaac
Atwater, Editor. New York: Munsell & Co., publishers,
1893, page 1069.

The portrait on page 34 and the house on page 44 are copied
from the first atlas of Minnesota: *An Illustrated Historical
Atlas of the State of Minnesota* published by A. T. Andreas in
1874.

The "birds eye view" on page 98, and the advertisement on
page 125 appear in the *Northwest Magazine* of April, 1886,
pages 39 and 45.

The drawing on page 91 is from a volume entitled: *We Present
a Collection of Seventy-five Sketches of St. Paul Citizens*
by Frank Wing, published in St. Paul in 1925.

The maps on pages 29, 93, and 152 are from an *Atlas of the Environs of St. Paul* published by G. M. Hopkins of Philadelphia in 1886. The map on page 12 is from a *Plat Book of the City of St. Paul, Minn. and Suburbs* published by G. M. Hopkins Company of Philadelphia in 1916.

The bank note on page 35 is found in a *Scrapbook documenting Junior Pioneer Association activities, St. Paul 1896-1936*, a two volume set located in the Library of the Minnesota Historical Society.

The poem *"The Lay of Nina Clifford"* has been circulating in typescript for years, but as far as I know, it has never been printed uncensored before.

All these illustrations were skillfully copied from originals by Eugene Becker of the Minnesota Historical Society in his usual excellent manner.

The cover illustration is the street where "I" live.